SELL YOURSELF

A Unique and Effective Approach to Selling Products, Services and Ideas

by William M. Saleebey, Ph.D.

Mentor Publishing

SELL YOURSELF

A Unique and Effective Approach
to Selling Products, Services and Ideas

By William M. Saleebey, Ph.D.

Published by
Mentor Publishing
1453-A Fourteenth Street
Santa Monica, CA 90404

Printed in the United States of America
Library of Congress Catalog Card Number: 94-75925
ISBN: 0-9640821-8-7

Editor: Nomi Kleinmuntz
Book/Cover Design: One-On-One Book Productions

I would like to dedicate this book to my parents, Bill and Selma Saleebey, who have always been supportive of me and my pursuits. Their lives and example serve as a constant source of inspiration. If everyone was as loving, honest, and hard-working as they are, this world would be a better place. I love them dearly, and thank them for their continued encouragement.

ABOUT THE AUTHOR

Dr. William Saleebey is the foremost expert on the psychological approach to the sales process. His background and extensive training enable him to combine the valuable skills of a successful sales professional, counselor, consultant, and learning specialist. He has developed a unique orientation to selling that is perfectly tailored for the modern salesperson.

He is currently Regional Sales Manager for the Mayflower Corporation. Saleebey has twice received the Salesperson of the Year award from Mayflower Transit Company. He is a respected lecturer and sales trainer, and an Adjunct Professor of Sales and Business for the University of Phoenix. He is also a partner in Focus for Success, which specializes in customized trainings for corporations and education. He is married and lives in Southern California with his wife and two teenage sons.

TABLE OF CONTENTS

ACKNOWLEDGEMENTS

This project could not have been accomplished without assistance and inspiration from others. I am sincerely grateful to the following individuals, without whom this book would have been only a dream.

Larry Whittet taught me how to sell, and provided me with numerous insights into the sales process. More importantly, he believed in me, taking me under his wing when I was floundering. His contributions to my career development have been tremendous. As my partner in Mentor Publishing, he is instrumental in the publication of this book.

My sales assistant, Linda Chavez, has helped me in more ways than she probably realizes. In our ten-year working relationship, she has had an ongoing influence upon my development and success.

My editor, Nomi Keinmuntz, assisted me greatly in improving the overall quality of the manuscript. Her knowledge of the English language is quite impressive. But more importantly, her gentleness and kindness were appreciated.

Appreciation also goes to my niece, Greta Lindholm for proofreading assistance and support.

I owe a debt of gratitude to Carolyn Porter and Alan Gadney of One-On-One Book Production and Marketing for taking the manuscript and preparing it for printing. In addition, they provided me with numerous useful ideas on design and marketing.

Living with a writer can be very difficult. At times, I am moody, driven, compulsive, noisy and generally a pain in the rear to live with. My family was not only tolerant, but very encouraging to me in the long and winding road to publication. My sons Billy and Colin were exemplary in their attitudes and behavior in dealing with a work in progress. Marie, my wife, never wavered in her support and encouragement of me and this project. I owe all of them much gratitude.

INTRODUCTION

Why should you read this book? What will you get out of it? Can you spare the time? How is this book different from other how-to-sell books? You should read this book because it discusses the most critical components of the selling process. If you understand, remember, and apply these concepts, YOU WILL BE SUCCESSFUL IN YOUR SALES CAREER. You will get out of it as much as you need and want. If you are new to sales, you will find a vast reservoir of useful information. You will get a realistic sense of what selling is, and you will learn specific techniques to improve your sales performance. You must make the time not only to read, but to ponder and practice new habits.

If you have been in sales for a while but are not reaching your potential, then this book can assist you as well. You might need to rethink your ideas about sales. Those of you with experience will more readily identify the situations and concepts. The reason that some salespeople are not successful is that their basic ideas about the sales process are simply incorrect or outdated. They need to take a fresh, more dynamic view of selling. The new perspective I offer here emphasizes an individual's personal style and the development of a high level of empathy for the buyer.

My primary focus is more upon professional, long-term sales. However, those selling almost anything part-time can derive something useful here. I refer to my personal sales experience many times. However, many of the concepts and principles will apply to your specialty. The basic process of sales can be understood by an in-depth study of one or several specific fields. Unique variations dictated by your specialty must be supplied by you. As you go through this book, you need to carefully consider the exact nature of your personality, your product/service, and your typical customers.

In fact, it is totally up to you as to how much you can benefit from this book. I provide you with the information. You must apply that information to your actual situation. You must accurately assess your current work habits, personal appearance, and skill level in order to improve your overall performance. You need to be very honest in your continuing appraisal of yourself. If you have difficulty in self-assessment, ask for honest feedback from someone you trust.

There is another potential difficulty that I will warn you about. If your sales manager, boss, or company has considerably different ideas from those presented here, then you could find yourself in conflict. If the ideas in this book ring true to you, you might have to either attempt to reeducate your sales manager (not always easy with the egos involved) or try to get yourself into a situation more compatible with your philosophy of sales.

If any of the ideas in this book are uncomfortable to you, you can choose not to implement them. However, before you abandon any of these ideas, ask yourself if you are willing to change to be successful. This might present a difficult decision. It is my hope that you select the philosophy, ideas, and techniques presented in this book. They *will* lead to success. If you want to give it a try, then read on. You have nothing to lose, and very much to gain from its content.

Sales training has typically been associated with certain assumptions about persuasion and earning money. In the past, the emphasis has been more on a "hard sell," using manipulation of the prospective customer. These traditional notions need to be reexamined in light of many critical aspects of modern society and the findings in the field of Psychology.

Salespeople are facing potential customers who are more sophisticated, saturated with sales efforts, and cynical than ever before. This book offers a synthesis of the major characteristics of successful salespeople. It does not provide cookbook scripts to be rote memorized and applied in pressured, manipulative, or dishonest ways. Rather, it presents psychological tools to assist you in achieving success through a personalized application.

You must honestly assess your current techniques and basic personality in order to determine what changes are necessary to improve your sales performance. Certain things can be taught. Others are inborn or instinctive. My approach allows you to make changes in accordance with the limits of your own personal comfort and motivational levels. Regardless of your personality, you can develop a successful approach to selling. As you read this book, you will gain many valuable ideas, the *essence* of sales. It is vital that you apply these ideas diligently and consistently in order to attain high levels of productivity. You need to identify your weakest areas and make sincere efforts to strengthen them. But not all of the skills that are discussed need to be at the highest levels of functioning. Your stronger areas can compensate for your weaker ones. Laziness might be overcome by efficiency and high closing ratios. It is quite simple: *use the ideas you find in this book and you will achieve success in your sales career.*

Success in sales depends upon many diverse factors. Not all of these factors are directly related to sales ability. For example, the state of the economy, the demand for your particular products or services, and the quality of the company that you are representing can either assist or hinder your sales efforts. There are numerous factors outside of your direct control that can influence your success levels. However, this book focuses more on the factors that you can directly control.

There are many different types of sales careers and selling situations. It is not within the scope of this book to analyze each specific type. However, I will discuss various categories of selling. It is up to you to make appropriate applications. The most basic breakdown is that of products and services. That is, most of you will either sell some type of product or some type of service. Outside of an actual sales career, you might be involved in a variety of sales situations, such as the following:

❖ Persuading your teenagers to drive carefully.

❖ Getting your family to agree with your vacation plans.

❖ Lobbying for a legislative change.

❖ Convincing a homeowners group about the hazards of a proposed commercial development.

❖ Convincing your sales manager to expand your territory.

Sales is everywhere. Everyone must become a salesperson at one time or another. Whether you are a full-time, commissioned salesperson or just sell occasionally or informally, you can use these ideas and techniques to improve your lifestyle and get what you want out of life.

Most of the basic concepts presented here apply to general sales situations. For example, personal appearance, though it will differ from situation to situation, is always important in sales. A discussion of repeat business account selling might not apply to a shoe salesman in a shopping mall. Organizational skills are always important, but are more critical in paper intensive situations.

You might be wondering about how or why I decided to write this book. Let me discuss a bit about the genesis of these ideas. Sales is a second career for me. I was an educator for ten years prior to becoming a salesperson. I taught a variety of Psychology, Counseling, and Education courses at the college and graduate school levels. I hold a doctorate in Educational Psychology from the University of California at Los Angeles. I became a salesperson in 1984 for Mayflower Moving and Storage, Inc., of Los Angeles California.

I did not have any formal sales training. When I joined Mayflower, I was given some basic ideas by my sales manager and advised to take the Dale Carnegie sales course. I went to an introductory session and decided that I was not particularly comfortable with the approach. Over the next couple of years, I was able to teach myself most of what I will present in this book. My primary purpose in writing this book is to share my ideas with you in order for you to improve your results. If you are not selling up to your potential, then you will find ideas here that will immediately assist you. You can read the entire book or go directly to the chapters that apply to you. Again, it is not enough to understand these concepts. You must apply them in order to see appreciable results.

I began my sales career in 1984 by selling household moves to individual families on a C.O.D. basis, running an average of five appointments per day. My initial performance could best be described as average. I didn't really enjoy doing that type of selling. In 1985 I began selling commercial office moving in the greater Los Angeles area. A veritable building boom in the mid-1980s, coupled with a highly transient business community provided me with tremendous opportunities to sell; Los Angeles is the top market for commercial moving in the United States. In terms of my company's experience and reputation (including the Mayflower name), and the market, things were working in my favor. If I couldn't sell under those conditions, then I couldn't sell.

Let me explain a little bit about my business. People have to move for a variety of reasons. Therefore, I am not convincing them to move. The normal circumstance was that a person would look in the phone book, call three or four potential movers for estimates, or bids, and then select one to be their mover. In an estimate situation, it is important to be both accurate and price-competitive. In some cases that presented a major challenge. I would enter a sales situation as a combination moving counselor/consultant, estimator, salesman, and corporate relocation manager (my official title). Prospective customers varied widely in their knowledge of the moving industry and their expectations of a moving company or its representative (me).

After introductions and a brief questioning period, I would conduct a survey of the items to be moved. It should be noted that all phases of a sale can be critical to the ultimate close. The introduction and ensuing first impressions, the type of questions I ask, and the care or detail that I take during the survey can greatly influence the decision to buy or not to buy. Many salespeople underestimate the importance of initial meetings to the ultimate sale. After the survey, I would calculate an estimate or guaranteed cost of services, using a formula based on cubic footage and past experience. Depending upon the size and complexity of the move, I would either make a sales presentation at that time or arrange to return after I had prepared a formal sales proposal with references and appropriate background material. Ideally, I would be dealing with the decision maker. In that case, I would know what the potential customer's criteria were for making the decision about whether or not to use my services.

In the early part of my sales career, I was exposed to some of the more traditional approaches to sales, such as those of Dale Carnegie and Tom Hopkins. While these approaches have had positive results with many salespeople, I have some fundamental differences with them. Primarily, my objections relate to the rote-memory-type scripts, the overly structured questioning, and above all the manipulative, often coercive style. Motivational approaches are helpful to beginning salespeople, but not sufficient to insure sales success in a long-term career.

Because of my educational training in the field of Psychology, I was developing my own personal philosophy of sales from the moment I began selling. The process of selling and what made people successful fascinated me. I have strong opinions about human behavior based upon years of study and experience. These ideas were shaped both by my academic training and experience. My approach to sales emphasizes the development of a unique individual style based on self-awareness. While traditional approaches often ignore the uniqueness of sales styles, it is the heart of my method. What does this mean in practice? To begin with, you must spend considerable time developing self-awareness—that is, who you really are as a person. Some examples of this are your pace, motivational priorities, outgoingness, attention to detail, love of people (or lack of it), level of self-confidence, and level of intelligence. Specifically, you need to have an understanding of your basic personality and characteristics. How do you do this? For me, it has been a lifelong process, which was enhanced by a rigorous study and teaching of Psychology. The level of psychological knowledge and expertise that I possess is not necessary to achieve success in sales. I will provide you with the basics. It is up to you to fill in the blanks.

You will then be able to develop a sales style designed to enhance your strengths and minimize your weaknesses. Although you might want to compare yourself to others, your ultimate approach will be your own. Personal traits, such as friendliness, orderliness, verbal skills, and persistence are then honed and synthesized into a total approach to sales and the selling process. In addition, I believe that successful salespeople in the 1990s and into the future must develop an approach to sales that takes into account the fact that many potential customers are resistant to pushy, manipulative, and overly aggressive salespeople. Because of this, I suggest a style that is less aggressive than the prototype hood-smashing used-car salesman. Times have changed, and with the changes salespeople must adjust to increasingly sophisticated and overexposed customers.

This book presents the major principles and essence of successful selling. It allows beginning and experienced sales-people to examine their current techniques and attitudes toward the selling process. By an accurate assessment of strengths and weaknesses, you will improve your selling skills and achieve higher levels of success. There are many different avenues to success. Each of you must chart your own path based upon self-awareness. In the beginning, this process might be confusing or overwhelming. But with time and effort, the various components will fit together and make sense to you. Success in sales is not achieved overnight. Sales is best seen as a long-term career in which composite skills must be developed over a considerable period of time. By continuing to work hard and developing a variety of skills, you will see progress.

PART I
SOME BASICS

1

SELF-AWARENESS:
You and I

When I began in sales, I had several things in my favor. I was educated, articulate (over ten years as a college professor), confident, enthusiastic, and highly motivated. I had already been successful in previous endeavors. My knowledge of my field (moving) was largely experiential (fifteen years as a helper, packer, and driver). I had no formal sales training. However, my training in Psychology did provide considerable knowledge of human thought and behavior. I consider myself intelligent, I learn most things quickly and easily, and I get along well with a wide variety of people. I was thirty-six years old when I began in sales.

My sales-related knowledge of the industry was probably below average when I began (compared to my competitors). My wardrobe was makeshift at best. I could project confidence, but the fact was that I was a novice. My initial sales results reflected that fact. I made a lot of calls, but not a lot of sales. My closing ratio was approximately 30 percent.

During those early months in sales, I had several major problems that prevented me from being more successful. First of all, I just didn't have enough knowledge of the moving industry to convince people that my estimates were accurate or my company was the best. I also emphasized quantity over quality appointments, losing too many jobs because I didn't spend enough time or effort with certain customers. I didn't try to close some customers, relying instead on them to call back and book the move. There is a fine line between closing a sale and pushing too hard. In this case I didn't push hard enough. Another area of weakness was pricing. I simply didn't do what was necessary to be competitive. Related to that was my inability to ask the appropriate questions regarding buying motives and criteria for decision-making. In sum, I just wasn't getting the volume of business I should have been getting.

One of the most difficult aspects of selling is that when we are new to sales, we simply don't possess the knowledge base of many of our competitors. Only time and experience can alleviate this problem. Because of this, it is so important to be patient and not to give up before you give sales a chance. In addition, our inexperience and nervousness show. It's a wonder that we make any sales at all during the first few months! During this period of time, it is critical to be aware of any progress that we do make. We need to learn why people buy or don't buy from us, and to get as many selling opportunities as possible so that this learning process can be accelerated.

How do we become aware of who we are? Basically, self-awareness is a lifelong process. We might learn about ourselves by the friends we choose, our hobbies, how we spend our time, our preferences, habits, and a myriad of other things. We might be different people in different situations. We change, mature, and have times of profound insight into our "essential self." What drives us? Why do we work? Are we morning people or slow starters? Are we fast-paced or slow-paced? Do we maintain many or few personal relationships? Are we detailed, methodical, or careless? Are we better at speaking or listening?

Do we prefer being in an office or on the road? You can begin this process (or continue it if you already possess a moderate level of self-awareness) by answering the above questions. Effective salespeople know what makes them comfortable and uncomfortable. They act in accordance with that knowledge. They don't continually fight themselves or try to copy another person with a completely different personality. You will not become fully self-aware overnight. However, you need to exert continual effort to find out who you are so you can develop a sales approach that is compatible with your basic underlying personality.

Increased self-awareness leads to decreases in self-doubt and effort. Self-awareness allows us to accept our personality and basic work style. By knowing ourselves we can direct our full attention to securing and maintaining the type of business that is best suited to our needs and preferences. In my own case, I prefer doing business with stable professional firms rather than industrial companies. Consequently, I am more successful selling to professional firms. My interest level is communicated to the prospective clients. This interest can take the form of genuine curiosity, specific questions about the company, or prior knowledge about the industry. Self-awareness allows us to identify more clearly the specific reasons why we make or do not make a particular sale. You cannot skip this step of becoming increasingly self-aware. Without it, you are doomed to mediocrity. With it, your potential is virtually limitless.

PERSONAL APPEARANCE
It Pays To Look Your Best

How important is your personal appearance? Very important! It is a well-known fact that people spend more time with others who are physically attractive than with those who aren't. We can't control the face and body we were born with, except perhaps with cosmetic surgery and exercise. However, we can control most of the factors that comprise our personal appearance. Clothes, hairstyle, makeup (for women), posture, jewelry (or lack of it), and grooming all contribute to the statement we make about who we are or the image we are trying to project. It is not my purpose nor area of expertise to tell you what specific style or colors to wear, how to cut your hair, or how much mascara to put on. However, there are certain principles that should be followed on a consistent basis. They are:

1. Dress and keep yourself neat at all times.

2. Wear colors that enhance your complexion.

3. Dress appropriately to your situation or environment.

4. Pay attention to details like lint, missing buttons, stains, ironing, and dirt. They matter.

5. Update and invest in your wardrobe. It will pay many dividends.

6. Consult a mirror frequently.

7. Pay attention to people's comments about your appearance or to whether any particular outfit is associated with success.

8. Sell or give away tattered, faded, or out-of-fashion clothes.

9. Keep your garments and body clean.

10. Be moderate in your use of colognes and perfumes.

By spending time, effort, and money on your personal appearance, you will create a more positive impression and increase your sales. Personal appearance is absolutely critical to success in sales. Don't let carelessness in this matter be a reason for losing a sales opportunity. Be the best you can be. Look your very best at all times.

YOUR PERSONA
Know the Images You Project

What images do you project to the many people you face? You need to understand the answer to this question in its many ramifications. Who are you? How do different people see you? Are you a pretty, petite, young woman, a large, intimidating "football player" type, an older guy who doesn't know how to dress, or a "technical" type?

I'll use myself as an example. After many years of relentless introspection, mirror watching, honest appraisal, wishful thinking, and countless discussions with others, I have developed a composite picture of who I am and who I am not to others. I am short (5'6"), stocky (175 pounds), olive-skinned, curly-haired (thinning with a bald spot in the back), have dark brown eyes, a hooked nose, full lips, am of full-blooded Lebanese descent, have a California dialect, am educated (Ph.D.), articulate, witty, sensitive, intense, and warm. If you don't know me, then all of that doesn't really tell you too much. It provides a rough image, but not much more.

Ethnically, I have been taken for Middle Eastern (all varieties), Italian, Greek, Mexican, Jewish, but not Swedish, Chinese, or Irish. I'm not tall by any American standard, but could appear of average height next to a very short person. It doesn't matter whether you have five or five hundred business suits. People see *you* on any given occasion, not your entire wardrobe. They don't know what else might be in your closet.

Certain items might lead to numerous assumptions about a

person: jewelry, makeup, hairstyle, or fragrances. Gold chains might mean nothing to you, but could conjure up an entire set of expectations to others. You need to be aware of the possible statement that you might be making by what you wear and how you present yourself. Ask friends and acquaintances about the image they receive from you. The goal is to present an image that is compatible with the company and product you represent. For example, if you sell shoes, then you should take extreme care in the footwear that you select to wear during business hours. By the same token, if you represent a conservative line of clothing, then you should dress conservatively yourself.

When you meet people, you might project one of a multitude of images. At times you can only speculate which one is active. It helps to ask people who will give you an honest answer if you are uncertain. If you are physically imposing, then an aggressive personality will only accentuate that aspect of your persona. If you are an extremely attractive and sexy woman, then flirtation could easily be misinterpreted. Don't assume that your innocent intentions are perceived as such by others. Above all, be yourself. Learn who you are and how others usually perceive you. By doing this, you will be able to modify your behavior and tone down extreme areas. If your physical appearance is wild or offbeat, then you can counteract it with some seriousness. In sum, you need to become increasingly aware of your persona and how it affects your performance.

PASSION
It Shows and It Works

Passionate people compel others to listen to and believe them. Passion, enthusiasm, drive, intensity, conviction, purpose— without these qualities a salesperson can easily appear average.

When people believe in and are excited about what they're doing (selling), it becomes contagious. Others want to become part of it.

In sales, it can be either the product or the process that creates the passion within the seller. For me, it continually fluctuates between the two factors. When neither is exciting to me, I probably lose more sales than I win. When both are driving me simultaneously, I am operating at my highest level of ability. What does this mean to salespeople? Quite simply, they should select a product or service that is intrinsically interesting to them. We should sell what we like and know, something that we can become passionate about.

I entered the sales profession more by accident than as a conscious career decision. At that time, I never imagined how ideally sales fit my personality or how excited I would become about it. I had years of experience as a mover, and selected moving sales for that reason. I am not always excited about moving. That fact certainly hurts my sales performance at times. However, I am fascinated about the notions of change and transition, and love to see a major relocation executed. I am deeply interested in the sales process (which should be obvious by my writing this book).

The fact that I am an intense, passionate person has contributed to my sales performance. In our complex society, people are looking for some feeling, some drive, some spunk. People who are bored with their product are usually unable to convince others to become excited and buy from them. The word *intensity* has probably been overused. But it does apply to successful people in all fields. A forceful, determined person is usually successful. Passion cannot be taught. People who are passionate about what they do have the edge over bland, bored people. It is probably better to be passionate about the product and process than merely about making money. Money is only the by-product of a skilled, hard-working, intense salesperson's consistent effort.

EXERCISES

All of the knowledge and awareness in the world will be of minimal utility if not put into practice. The first step is hearing and seeing. The second step is understanding. The third step is remembering what you have learned. We are now at the critical fourth step, that of putting this information into practice. It is essential to your success to practice what you have learned. I realize it's difficult to change your habits and ways of doing things. But if you are not realizing your full potential, then there must be certain attitudes or behaviors that need to be changed. You are probably the best judge about your strengths and weaknesses. In fact, others might give you inaccurate feedback regarding this matter. Your first step is to look closely within yourself to determine exactly what you're thinking and doing. Then you can determine the nature and degree of change necessary to improve your current performance.

Exercise 1: Who Am I?

Prior to developing a sales strategy and accompanying techniques, you need to determine who you are. What motivates you, how do you spend your time, what makes you tick? For this first exercise, take out some blank paper. Then, at a time when your mind is free, write a brief autobiography. Describe yourself as you might to someone who has never met you. Don't assume anything. After you have written it, then go back and underline key words or things that you have mentioned more than once. Next, try to determine which of your characteristics have remained constant over the years and which might be changing. Keep these in mind as you begin to develop your own unique sales style.

Exercise 2: Strengths and Weaknesses

In this very important exercise you will be asked to list and analyze your major strengths and weaknesses as they might apply to sales. You should rank each of the following categories on a scale of 1 to 10, 10 being the highest. For example, if you feel that your product knowledge is virtually nonexistent, then you would give yourself a 1 next to product knowledge. Be honest, and really look carefully at yourself. Rank the following categories:

——Level of Self-Awareness	——Being Organized
——Friendliness	——Honesty/Integrity
——Need for Structure & Direction	——Thoroughness
——Personal Appearance (including looks, grooming, & wardrobe)	——Patience
——Promptness	——Verbal Ability
——Cold Calling	——Persistence
——Product Knowledge	——Charisma
——Financial Motivation	——Flexibility
——Sense of Humor	——Sensitivity
——Writing Ability	——Competitiveness
——Listening Ability	——Learning Ability
—— Ego-Strength/Self-Confidence	——Closing Ability
——Interest Level in Product/Service You Represent	

19

After you have ranked all of the above categories, group them into levels 1-3, 4-7, and 8-10. By doing this, you can assess strong, average, and weak areas. Then you must try to improve on your weak and average areas. The strong areas must be maintained, and you can consider how your strengths can be utilized to compensate for weaknesses. It should be noted that some of the above characteristics can be easily changed with effort. An example of this would be product knowledge. However, something like competitiveness might be less subject to change. You will not change everything overnight. The goal here is to first become aware of your basic strengths and weaknesses, and then to make a long-term effort to improve.

THE IMPORTANCE OF A POSITIVE ATTITUDE AND APPROACH

People respond far better to positive people than to negative people. Stay positive. Your attitude has much to do with your ultimate success. If you keep your attitude positive and optimistic, then you will generate more response. This doesn't mean that you should be a Pollyanna and not face problems or low closing ratios. But rather, that you should maintain a pleasant demeanor and a basically positive attitude and approach to your work and life.

When you meet someone, you get an immediate impression about whether he or she is positive or negative. Potential customers receive salespeople in the same way. If you are cheerful and upbeat you will get better results than if you are glum and somber. When you are in an extremely bad mood, it is probably best not to attempt to sell if you can do some paperwork instead. By having and projecting a positive attitude and approach, you will not only improve your sales results but also the overall quality of your life. People will want to be in your presence. And that will, in turn, lead to additional sales and potential contacts.

2

YOU
AND THE COMMISSION
SALES PROCESS

E arning a living on a strict commission basis can be a bit intimidating for some people. "What if I don't make it?" is a common fear. "I need a guaranteed salary," say others about a career. The following section addresses the most common form of sales, that of commission or percentage compensation. *Commission sales is not for everyone.* There are not always financial guarantees offered for the initial period of employment. However, there are few limits as to how much you can earn. It is a definite risk, but one with the clear potential of substantial income and career satisfaction.

Who, then, is cut out for commission sales? There are certain common characteristics that successful salespeople possess to varying degrees. Generally, those who succeed in sales careers like contact with a variety of people. They prefer working with other people over working primarily with machines or ideas. They are typically self-confident, sometimes to the point of egotism. They want to make considerable sums of money for their efforts, being rewarded for superior talent.

There is a tendency for them to be competitive—they like to win. Successful salespeople know how to motivate themselves. They function effectively in low-structured conditions requiring minimal supervision. So far, does this sound like a description of you? How many of the above-mentioned factors apply to you? Are you being honest with yourself? Are you willing to pay the price and take the time to achieve success in your sales career?

Now we turn to the other side of the coin. That is, to people who are uncomfortable in a straight commission situation. First of all, any type of sales is probably not for people who prefer a work environment that is structured and controlled by a supervisor. These people prefer the security and predictability of a guaranteed salary over the potential of higher commission earnings. The fluctuation of income would probably bother them. They do not really like the idea of having to be constantly self-motivating, preferring instead to work with machines, objects, or ideas. There are other common traits in individuals who are basically uncomfortable in commission sales: shyness, lack of motivation, lack of confidence, poor verbal ability, lack of assertiveness, fragile ego, impatience, and low financial aspirations. In sum, people who don't succeed, or ever enter into commission sales in the first place, have difficulty with the uncertainty associated with selling.

Sales can be highly competitive, stressful, and subject to peaks and valleys. Successful salespeople tend to be bothered less by these factors than others. In fact, some enjoy and thrive on them. The successful ones realize that with skill, consistent effort, and self-improvement the possibility of failure decreases. Others are simply not inclined to pursue sales over a prolonged period of time. They might be attracted to the idea of big money or a flexible schedule with minimal supervision or accountability. But they are often unwilling or unable to pay the price of achieving those perceived benefits. Most successful sales professionals like the possibility of virtually limitless income. They prefer being compensated on the basis of effort and ability rather than number of hours worked. Conversely, people who leave sales also like the idea of substantial commissions, but have difficulty tolerating inconsistent paychecks. Not all sales positions are straight commission. For people who might not resonate to pure commission selling, salary plus commission might be a preferable option.

Sales often requires you to work alone, make endless cold calls, and wait months or even years for sufficient rewards. You might face an entire week of blank schedule, just waiting for you to fill it in. This lack of structure and specific tasks creates a different type of stress than a demanding manager. How do you deal with large blocks of free time? The answer to that question reveals much about your ultimate success in commission sales. The successful salesperson learns how to schedule a balanced week (new business, repeat business, administration, pros- pecting, self-improvement) during both peak and slow periods. There is a real art to effective scheduling. We don't always know how long a given appointment will take, how much traffic will be present, or what other factors will become involved.

Most people would like to receive a large commission payment, but few are willing to earn it. It takes a variety of skills and attitudes that only few people possess to any degree. As in other aspects of selling, you can compensate for weaknesses with your strengths. But if your basic personality is incompatible with the requirements of commission sales, then your stay in sales will be short. Before committing yourself to a sales career, take a deep and honest look at the above issues.

COMMON MYTHS ABOUT THE SALES PROCESS

One of the major reasons that beginning salespeople struggle longer than necessary is that they hold onto myths about the sales process. These myths are simply mistaken notions about what it takes to be successful in a sales career. Most of these myths will be mentioned later in this book. But they bear repeating, further consideration, and remembering. They are as follows:

❖ **Myth 1**—*Sales is really the art of deception.*

> On the contrary, most effective salespeople are honest individuals who are committed to truth and integrity.

❖ **Myth 2**—*You should try to persuade prospective customers even after they have made up their mind not to buy from you.*

> Persistence is one thing, but carried too far it becomes obnoxious and counter-productive. Sales successes know when to retreat and accept a no answer, at least for the time being.

❖ **Myth 3**—*Sales careers provide large paychecks with minimal efforts.*

> Nothing could be further from the truth. In fact, it takes considerable, sustained effort and skill to attain substantial commissions on a consistent basis.

❖ **Myth 4**—*Sales really just involves being a nice, friendly person.*

> Although it is necessary to have a pleasant personality, it is not sufficient. You cannot rely on personality to sell at a high level.

❖ **Myth 5**—*Once you get established in sales, it's PARTY TIME.*

> Not so! You need to work on a consistent basis long after you have achieved initial success to keep your sales levels high.

❖ **Myth 6**—*After you have secured a repeat business account, you can let your inside support people take over.*

This can be a major mistake. It is true that inside people can handle orders and basic paperwork, but you should never ignore your accounts. Your customers need attention, communication, and *your* personal touch. You are the reason they bought from your company in the first place.

❖ **Myth 7**—*Salespeople should be all business.*

It is very important to focus on business, but not without sincere greetings, some human interaction, and your personal warmth. Never forget the *person* who is your customer. If you do, you will lose that customer. It's okay to lighten up a bit.

❖ **Myth 8**—*Once you are established in sales, you'll never have to prospect again.*

Although this might be true in rare cases, it is more often the case that prospecting to some degree is necessary long into your sales career. However, it gets easier as you become more experienced.

❖ **Myth 9**—*Don't get involved in the personal lives of your customers or inside support people.*

Why not? Though there might be some sensible limits and boundaries to your relationships, you should communicate as deeply as seems prudent.

❖ **Myth 10**—*If you have the skills and put forth the effort, you can be highly successful in a short period of time.*

I really wish this were true. Unfortunately, most people must struggle for at least a couple of years before reaching consistent levels of sales success.

Review this list of myths whenever you're in a rut or selling slump. You will probably find one or more of them that you still believe. Test them out for yourself; don't take them on faith. Ultimately, you'll want to get rid of them. They are quite dangerous, and will hold you back from reaching your full potential.

SELLING YOURSELF

It has been said that sales is really just a matter of selling yourself. You begin any sales transaction by introducing yourself to the prospective customer. First impressions are formed, and much of the final decision can already have been made after the first meeting. Many customers state flatly that they buy almost totally on the basis of the personality of the salesperson. Personality alone cannot substitute for an inferior product, service, or company, but it can have a tremendous impact on the buyer's decisions.

There are many things that you can convey to a prospective buyer about yourself that influence decisions. Some of them are:

1. *Friendliness*—Are you the kind of person who is amiable and pleasant to be around? Are you cheerful, positive, and courteous?

2. *Reliability*—Do you do what you say you're going to do? Are you prompt for meetings, deliveries, and other commitments? Can you be counted on to deliver on your promises?

3. *Integrity*—Are you honest and fair in your business dealings? Can you be trusted to handle an account without being monitored? Do you truly care and have the customer's interests in mind at all times?

4. *Commitment*—Do you plan to stay with your company and your accounts for several years, or are you only out to make some fast money?

5. *Power*—Do you exert enough clout within your own company to settle potential monetary disputes, service problems, and mistakes?

You represent your product and company with everything you say and do. If you present yourself with professionalism, knowledge, and honesty, then it will probably be assumed that your product/service are high quality. If you look good, sound good, and act accordingly, then you become the best possible advertisement for your company. You are always selling yourself. Thus, you must continue to improve yourself to be the best you can be.

SETTING YOUR GOALS

Setting life and career goals is a strong motivational strategy for salespeople. There are two basic types of goals: general and specific. It is wise to have both types of goals for yourself. In the beginning of your sales career, it is sometimes difficult to set specific goals. However, you should have some benchmark that you are shooting for. For example, in my field the target is $1 million per year. Million dollar bookers get much respect in the moving industry. At 8 to 10 percent commission, you earn from $80,000 to $100,000 per year, plus benefits and expenses at the $1 million level.

You don't have to set goals that are overly difficult to achieve, nor give yourself an unrealistic time-frame in which to achieve them. There are many ways to set goals. You can set them around the number of contacts you make with new customers per week. Or you could set monthly rather than yearly goals. Another type of goal could be improving your ratio of closing sales. Your company probably has quotas set for you. But the most important goals are the ones you set for yourself. Don't get discouraged or stop working if you fail to achieve your goals. You need to determine the barriers or weaknesses that are preventing you from reaching them.

Goal setting is a continual process. When you reach one goal, you need to set another one to give yourself some target to aim for. Intermediate goals provide you with some immediate gratification until you attain your ultimate goals.

The goals that we set for ourselves are very personal. If you set a goal of selling $500,000 per year (at 8 percent commission), and are satisfied earning $40,000, then you should not be unduly influenced by people who are selling in excess of $1 million. The same is true of other endeavors. For example, some golfers are perfectly satisfied playing in the 90s. Others are very upset if their score is over 80. Our goals have a powerful influence on our behavior. Take care in setting them, revise them as necessary, and keep improving your skills.

The level of your goals strongly influences how hard you work and how much you must develop your selling skills. If your goals are very high, then your skills and work ethic must match them. But, setting them too high, too quickly, can leave you frustrated and discouraged if you don't achieve them. Conversely, if your goals are low, then you can reach a comfort zone with less effort and skills. It is totally up to you. No one else can tell you how successful you should be.

Exercise 3: Whom Do You Buy From?

One of the best ways to get in touch with the sales process is to carefully consider your own buying habits. Think about every situation in which you confront a salesperson. Why do you buy something? What do you look for in a product, service, and salesperson? Conversely, what turns you off about salespeople?

It is probably true that you are developing a sales approach that includes components from your positive list (that is, who you buy from) and eliminates negative features.

Even though your buying motives may not be typical of the "average" person, they can provide valuable information for you. What cues do you attend to when someone is trying to sell you something? What things are not important to you? When you are making a buying decision, what primary factors do you weigh? Answer the following questions honestly.

1. What is the first thing you notice about a salesperson?

2. What things tend to impress you about a salesperson?

3. Do you usually do a lot of shopping around before you buy something?

4. Are you more concerned with the person you are buying from or the written guarantees?

5. Do you believe most of what you hear from a salesperson?

6. Is there any pattern to your buying decisions?

7. Do you make your decisions more on "gut feelings" or a logical "spread sheet" type of comparison?

8. Is it important that the salesperson establish a rapport with you?

9. What things tend to turn you off about a salesperson?

10. In general, what are the main reasons you decide to buy something?

Did any patterns emerge from this exercise? Were there certain things that you mentioned more than once? Do you feel that your approach to sales is consistent with your own preferences and buying motives? When you get into a rut or a slump, reconsider your own buying patterns. It might assist you in getting back on track.

Exercise 4: Goal-Setting

❖ What are your life and career goals?

❖ Why are you pursuing a sales career?

❖ Why are you reading this book?

❖ What drives you?

❖ What is important to you?

❖ What are your priorities?

❖ What do you want in the near future?

❖ What are your long-term life goals?

Obviously, goals are important aspects of human motivation. Goals impel us to act. If we had no goals at all, we would be inert masses of flesh. But instead we are driven variously toward riches, serenity, power, fame, or security. You need to get strongly in touch with the basic needs and desires that drive you.

❖ Are your goals general or very specific?

❖ Do you have a clear visual picture of your future?

❖ Or, are you merely trying to do your best and waiting to see what happens?

❖ Do you usually achieve your goals in life?

❖ Do you think you know what it takes to reach them?

Well, I've asked you a lot of questions. Now I want you to

answer the above questions in the form of a written goal statement. Use any format you want. You can simply go back to the beginning of this exercise and list the questions, along with your answers. Another approach is to write a short essay that encompasses answers to the above questions. I think you'll find that the results will provide you with some additional insight into your goals and motivational patterns.

In the second part of this exercise, I want you to restate your general and specific, short-term and long-term career and life goals. Attach monetary values to the goals. For example, develop sales projections for the next five years, month by month. Remember, the most important step toward reaching the goals is *hard work*.

3

THE MENTOR
SOMEONE WHO
SHOWS THE WAY

A mentor is a teacher who guides a new salesperson through the major steps necessary to achieve success in sales. In addition, a mentor provides continual feedback regarding the progress of the aspiring salesperson. The mentor could be the sales manager or a high-producing salesperson who takes the time and effort to share effective attitudes and sales techniques. A mentor also provides encouragement, positive reinforcement, constructive criticism, ideas, and any information that will assist the trainee.

In my own sales career, I was very fortunate to have a true mentor. Larry Whittet, my supervisor, led the way for me, both with words and example. As my sales manager, he provided me with numerous insights into the sales process and transportation industry. He was always willing to talk with me at length about my self-doubts, sales situations, and this enigmatic career we had chosen.

Larry was genuinely interested in my progress. He constantly asked me at the beginning of my career: "Are you sure you want to do this?" "Do you still like this?" We worked together, and he provided me with much useful feedback. Primarily, he told me to be more specific and detailed in my approach. I had been too vague in the past. He encouraged and applauded me frequently for my cold calling and phone techniques. He would say often, "Keep making those calls and the business will be there." He answered all of my questions in great detail. I was only seeking pearls of wisdom, and he was giving me necklaces.

Larry had risen from a truck driver to one of the top-producing office moving salespeople in the greater Los Angeles area. He did it through hard work, a judicious use of references and referrals, continued enthusiasm, a thorough product knowledge, ownership in our company, and consummate professionalism. His style is somewhat different from mine. However, I was able to observe him over a period of time and borrow those aspects of his approach which fit my philosophy and personal style. He is strong, convincing, and sincere. His track record is impeccable, which leads to substantial referral business. Without Larry as a mentor and consistently positive role model, I might still be floundering.

Sales can be a lonely profession. A competent mentor provides a needed source of communication and support. We need not be alone. It assists us to know what our mentor did (or does) in similar situations. The ideal mentor provides training (knowledge), moral support, guidance, encouragement, and ideas for generating and maintaining business. A mentor cares about your success, and does whatever is possible to assist you in achieving your goals.

Finding a mentor can occur in a variety of ways. You might

be as fortunate as I was to have someone who takes you under their wing. Another way to find an appropriate mentor is to ask many questions about the sales process of people whom you respect. In any case, seek help and ask questions.

One of the main reasons for the premature attrition of new salespeople is weak training and management. People new to sales usually need much guidance. They need moral support, encouragement, specific direction, and ideas. A mentor really should also be a role model. In many instances it is the *sales manager* who serves as mentor to aspiring salespeople. I have observed two basic types of sales managers: those who sell and those who don't sell. The ones who sell usually have a more immediate, practical knowledge of the sales process. Those who don't sell are often too theoretical or general and might have lost touch with the "real world" of the modern customer.

The essence of effective sales management is communication. A beginning salesperson should have the opportunity to be guided by a mentor who is sensitive to his or her unique personality, selling style, and goals. A mentor gives the beginner the belief that success is possible. In addition, the mentor teaches and provides guidance regarding techniques that will lead to success. The ultimate goal should be independence. But until you learn the basics, training by a mentor is necessary for true success. The mentor should be generous with information about the sales process. The more that is shared, the better.

PROFILES

The profiles throughout this book are about actual individuals employed in the sales profession. They represent a broad range in terms of age, levels of experience and success, type of product/service, and situation. I want you to read each one of them with the intention of finding situations or personality characteristics with which you can identify. One of the major tenets of this book is that due to the uniqueness of human personality and experience there is a wide variety of effective sales approaches. There is not just one way, but many. It is up to you to build your own model of success. You need to identify your strengths and weaknesses in order to do this effectively.

I will present the most dominant characteristics of each individual in order to illustrate my points. The profiles are not complete life histories or personality analyses, but basic characteristics and tendencies that impact heavily upon sales performance.

PROFILE 1—Larry Whittet, the Mentor
A Portrait of a True Professional Sales Success

Without any doubt, Larry Whittet was my primary role model and sales mentor. He is the person I would look to in critical sales situations for suggestions and answers to my questions. This case study includes many of the characteristics possessed by sales successes.

Upon first meeting him, nothing seems extraordinary about Larry. He is pleasant looking, average in physique, conservatively attired, and casual. Nothing is really evident from the first impression that this is a true sales success story. Larry is very personable. Soft-spoken and down-to-earth, he is an excellent conversationalist. His sincerity and genuine interest in people are evident from the start.

The initial impression that Larry creates with most people provides a tremendous foundation leading to the ultimate sale and repeat business. However, it is the things he does after the first meeting that stamp him as a true professional sales success. His personality gets him started; his skills and effort keep him going.

He knows the moving and storage business backward, forward, and inside out. His product knowledge is superior. As an owner of Mayflower, he can make and honor commitments that other competitors might not be able to match. Larry possesses a strong determination to secure the order. He determines, usually quite accurately, what he needs to say and do to be awarded the business. Then he leaves no stone unturned in his quest for the final close. He truly focuses upon the pertinent details, and makes those facts his building blocks.

How does he do these things? First of all, by establishing a strong rapport with the potential customer, he lays the groundwork for direct and honest communication. Then he can determine along the way what his standing is in terms of the quest for the order. He asks direct questions, has great intuition based on experience about the criteria for buying decisions, and determines his course of action.

His use of referrals and references generates a significant amount of business. Not only does he have a vast list of references, but he knows which ones to highlight for specific situations. By doing a superior job over a period of twenty-three years, he has amassed a wide network of referrals, lead sources, and business contacts.

When problems arise, Larry's approach is to confront them directly and honestly. He has the skill to not only solve a problem, but to turn it into more business. He works diligently to improve the day-to-day operations of Mayflower. During a crisis he is usually calm and rational. He will ask numerous questions rather than jumping to a hasty response.

Thoroughness is another of Larry's characteristics. His proposals and sales presentations demonstrate a complete command of the various aspects of the customer's situation. He takes much time and reflection to derive his price quotations and the formats of proposals.

On the phone, he is never rushed. He will take as much time as the customer needs to talk. Again, his amiability is endearing to most customers. He portrays the image of a person who truly cares about what happens to the customer. And he does.

In sum, Larry Whittet has become an extraordinary sales success by applying most of the principles described in this book. His several strongest traits compensate for the couple of weaker ones. He works hard, consistently, and continues to apply the techniques that have made him successful. He maintains an apparent innocence that seem to contradict his enormous success. If every salesperson could have a mentor like him, there would be many more successful salespeople.

4

ESTABLISHING RAPPORT
Tнє Goldєn CARPET
To SALES

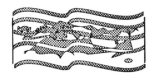

Rapport—without it you have nothing! I realize this sounds like an extreme statement, but it's true. A salesperson *must* establish rapport with prospective customers. What is rapport? Essentially, it is a comfortable state shared by two people, of knowing and liking one another, a genuine connection on some personal level. Rapport means that something has been established, a mutual recognition of the other person as a unique individual. We can develop rapport by deepening our levels of communication beyond superficial conversation.

How can we establish rapport? One good way is to find out some pertinent facts about the other person—occupation, family status, hobbies, life situation, personal relationships, pets, topics of interest. This process should come from a genuine interest in the other person, not a mechanical discussion strictly designed to get business. When we have established rapport with someone, we then feel more comfortable asking them direct questions. They have more of a tendency to treat us fairly and care about us. There then exists a sort of *bond* that we don't have with strangers. Of course, there are different levels of rapport. We have more rapport with our spouse or best friend than the mailman (I hope). The salesperson who deepens the levels of rapport makes it more difficult for the customer not to buy. We are talking here about a comfort level that makes doing business easier and more fun. On another dimension, we feel better about giving top level service to people we care about.

These lessons were taught to me by experience early in my life. My parents owned and operated a "variety" store (then called a *five and dime*) in the Los Angeles suburb of Pasadena. The name of the store was, appropriately enough, Saleebey's. My mother ran the counter cash register herself. She was much more than merely a clerk. She got to know her customers by name. In addition, she usually knew something about their lives and families. There was always a cheerful greeting for them. As she used to say, "They'd (the customers) come in for a ten cent spool of thread and chat for fifteen minutes." Life was slower then, and my parents believed that if you treated people honestly and kindly, then you would induce loyalty in them. People continued to do business with my parents more for their warmth and sincerity than any other single reason. And many of Saleebey's customers have remained personal friends some twenty-five years after the store was sold. They cared deeply for others, and are still reaping the benefits.

The ability to establish rapport is probably not teachable. You can't teach someone to care or to be warm. These qualities flow naturally from a genuine concern and love for others. We do it because we like people and are sincerely interested in their lives and well-being. Some people are highly successful in sales primarily because of their ability to establish positive rapport with customers.

When a salesperson skips the rapport-building stage to make a quick sale, most customers feel alienated. It is important to get down to business, but not in lieu of building rapport. Once some comfort level has been established, you should then proceed smoothly into the sales process. However, the person who is the customer should never be ignored. If they are made to feel more valued, more human, then they are more likely to buy.

Rapport is also quite important if problems arise. Many things can go wrong before, during, and after the consummation of a sale. If rapport has been established, then any difficulties can be directly addressed and solved in a more friendly environment. The customer might be willing to overlook minor problems if sufficient rapport has been developed. You must never forget the critical importance of rapport in the overall sales process. Without it you have nothing.

SOCIALIZING:
THE ART OF MIXING AND MINGLING

There is an old saying that it's not what you know but who you know that counts. Actually, both are important; you can't rely on your social contacts alone. But even with a great deal of knowledge and selling skill, you might be stymied in some situations if you don't know the right people. One way to get to know the right people is by being socially active. This could take the form of social clubs, service organizations, chambers of commerce, parents organizations, athletics, dancing, or cards. Whatever you do socially, it should be something you enjoy.

Contacts are vitally important in many sales situations. I have gotten considerable business just from friends' referrals. The best contacts are people who know and like you as a person first, and as a salesperson second. There are some salespeople who can attribute much of their success to the fact that they are very likable. People want to be around them, including doing business with them. Get involved with other people in social situations. Let them know what business you are in. But, be patient and get to know people a bit first before jumping into business. This is very important. Some beginning salespeople give out their business card before they even introduce themselves.

I have had a lot of success meeting people through my children's school and athletic activities. People who meet me through these activities get to know, like, and respect me long before they ever know that I'm in the moving business. The relationship is developed prior to any attempt at soliciting business.

Your business will grow by leaps and bounds if you are involved in meaningful social activities. If you are genuinely friendly and sociable, then people will want to give you their business. Don't force social contact with influential people. If you happen to meet them, try to refrain from talking business prematurely. The proper time will come, and you will be better off for having waited. Above all, be yourself. If you are not overly sociable, then don't just join organizations indiscriminately. Find an activity that you truly enjoy, and then you will probably get more involved in it.

PROFILE 2—Bob Eisele
Exceptional Product, Persuasiveness, and Personableness

Bob Eisele is a writer/producer. He has written numerous plays and screenplays over a twenty-five-year writing career. He was awarded the coveted Humanitas Award for an episode of the television program *Cagney and Lacey*. He is a truly talented writer with a broad range and depth.

In addition to Bob's writing talent, he has a dynamic personality and quick wit. For starters, his product is high quality. But without his sales ability gained from his training as a shoe salesman early on and his endearing personality, he might still be struggling over a manual typewriter. His ability to convince film executives of the worth of his work is exceptional. He created and fully executed his product. He totally believes in it and controls it. His knowledge of it is thorough and deeply internalized. There is no dependence on another person regarding the quality of his work.

Bob is a very personable, down-to-earth guy. He makes people feel immediately at ease with him through his sincerity and ever-present humor. People like him. He makes a habit of finding something out about everyone he meets. Being an attentive listener helps him not only in his writing but also in his sales.

Having a solid product and sparkling personality are helpful, but not sufficient to convince people to buy his work. He is also enthusiastic, convincing, and determined. His verbal communication skills enhance his highly developed writing skills. Another writer with similar writing skills might not have achieved a fraction of Bob's success without the ability to sell.

It might be said that some of the primary reasons (other than writing ability) for Bob's sales success cannot really be taught. However, if you possess them, you can develop them and use them to your advantage. Charm, wit, amiability, and persuasiveness all make it difficult for a prospective buyer to say no to you.

KNOWING THE RIGHT PEOPLE

You need to get in front of decision makers in order to make sales. In addition, you might need to know and cultivate a positive relationship with people who can exert a powerful influence upon the decision makers, in cases where the actual decision maker is unavailable to you. Don't get me wrong here. What you know is very important. But unless you present it to the right people, it can be wasted effort.

One of the most frustrating aspects of sales is when you make a wonderful presentation to a person who has absolutely no part in the final decision. You need to make every effort within reason to present your case directly to the decision maker. Find out who is making the final decision, and then ask for some time with him or her. You need to be very careful not to offend your initial contact (who might be an assistant or office manager) by asking to present your case directly to the decision maker. Use diplomacy at all times; if you offend a person with your directness or demands to speak to the decision maker, you could be denied from being considered at all.

Sometimes this issue can take on a different dimension. For example, let's say that you know the president of a corporation through your church. He has always been friendly to you and your family. But you are reluctant to ask him if he will help you get some business from his company. What you might do is to get him aside, tell him your situation, and ask him if he might introduce you to the appropriate person. At that point, he may volunteer to do more for you than that. You probably don't want to ask for too much, but don't be afraid to use his influence if it is offered to you.

When you happen to know people who exert power or influence, you need to be tactful and diplomatic in order to use that influence to secure business. Take your time. Don't ask for favors immediately. Perhaps the best approach is to inform them of your interest at the proper time, and then wait for them to make the next move. It might be necessary to remind them at some point. If and when they are able to help you, make sure to thank them for their assistance.

5

THE IMPORTANCE of BEING ORGANIZED

The Confessions of an Obsessive Compulsive

B eing organized is crucial to success in any endeavor. By staying organized, you know where to find what you need when you need it. Phone numbers, price quotations, specifications, directions, and other critical data are at your fingertips when you require them. It is helpful to take time and effort in the evening and/or the early morning (normally non-selling time) to put your mind and paperwork in order. Once your work is organized, then you are free to sell without worrying about these details. You will not be distracted by a lapse in memory or some other uncompleted tasks. Being organized must become a priority for you. Do not make the excuse that you are not an organized person. Become one. Organization is yet another piece in the puzzle of what makes people successful in sales careers. Customers are more likely to buy from salespeople who remember to write up their orders correctly and on time.

When a person is organized, it leads to promptness and clarity of thought. An organized person projects professionalism and integrity. So how can you get organized? You need to:

☐ Establish a system for filing proposals, client information, and other pertinent data.

☐ Keep and update records so you can respond quickly to the needs of your customers.

☐ Discard old, unnecessary paperwork.

☐ Clean out your desk and briefcase frequently.
Our minds work best when we rid them of irrelevant information. People with messy work areas tend to have messy minds, and they waste far too much time because of their disorganization.

☐ Maintain a daily and weekly calendar with a section for phone numbers and addresses. (This is like a bible for me.)

I attempt to keep with me or carefully file all of the pertinent information about pending and active business. I figure price quotations as soon as possible after my surveys. This allows me to concentrate fully on my next call. I do not let paperwork stack up on my desk. Through these techniques, I stay ahead of the many daily demands of my job.

All of these factors lead to clarity of thought, a positive self-image, and increased motivation to sell. In addition, you free up many selling hours by being highly organized. By projecting the image of an organized person, your chances to make sales increase. Customers respect people who are organized, have a good memory, and know where to find things.

How can you begin to become more organized? You should observe organized people and learn from them. Set aside time each day to organize yourself. This *must* become a major priority for you. If it isn't, you will simply never reach high levels of productivity. Experiment with various methods until you discover those with which you are the most comfortable. Develop a plan that is simple and workable. Don't try to change everything overnight. Modify your plan until it becomes a set of habits that are comfortable for you. Then stay organized, and see how your sales skyrocket.

Exercise 5—Getting and Staying Organized

In order to reach high levels of sales success, you need to get and stay organized. How can you do this? First of all, you need to identify the specific areas that you most need to improve. Time management, record keeping, neatness of your office or work space, filing, and client information are some common areas that need to be kept in order. Start by ranking yourself from 1 to 10 (10 being the highest) on those categories:

1. Time management

2. Record keeping

3. Neatness

4. Filing

5. Client Information

If you ranked yourself below 6 on any of these categories, then you need definite improvement. You can begin by setting aside some time, preferably nonselling time, to get yourself organized. You could start anywhere. For example, empty out your briefcase completely. Go through the contents and only put back the things that you absolutely need. File or purge nonessential items. This should be done at least once a week.

Next, you should rid your desk and office of unnecessary items. Dust, polish, and make your area one that is orderly. The order allows your mind to operate more clearly. You could then organize your clothes, discarding old or tattered garments. The entire process of organization can take a full day or more. But you will notice immediate results in terms of your attitudes and performance.

Do things your way. Don't be unrealistic about this process. You will not completely change your habits in a week or a month. But it is time to begin. Update phone numbers and addresses, centralize or computerize important data, and clean up your act. Everything should be included: your bedroom, your car, your office, your body. It might even be time to consider a new hairstyle. Once you have made the required changes, work on a daily basis to maintain them. You will see impressive results by staying more organized. It does make a difference.

PROMPTNESS: BE ON TIME ALL THE TIME

You must arrive on time! There are few legitimate excuses for being late. Tardiness makes a negative statement about you. It basically says that being on time is not important to you and that your commitment to your appointment is not being kept. With proper planning and setting of priorities, you can easily be on time 95 percent of the time or more. But in order to do this, promptness must move to the top of your priority list. You must plan carefully, allow for traffic and unforseen delays, and arrive on time or a few minutes early. Part of the problem for some people is simply a lack of awareness of what time it is. For others, it is poor judgment about how long various things take. Some people underestimate distances or overestimate their ability to travel without encountering traffic or quickly find a parking space.

I am talking about more than merely being prompt. By arriving early, you can relax, prepare yourself if necessary, and get oriented to your new environment. You won't have the frantic feelings of anxiety and discomfort caused by being late for an important appointment. An example is parents who drive their children to school habitually tardy or "at the bell." Tension levels rise, children might become unduly nervous, and there is no time to become oriented. Besides, most children enjoy playing with their friends before school.

I arrive for an important business appointment such as a presentation for a major relocation project preferably about fifteen minutes before the scheduled meeting. I can then check out the building for move conditions if that has not already been done. I will go to the restroom to check my appearance. But perhaps the most important thing is for me to collect my thoughts and do any last minute preparation. I then go to the meeting place and announce myself about five minutes prior to the actual appointment time.

It should be emphasized that besides the many ways in which you might benefit from being early, your customer is favorably impressed with punctuality. The image of a neatly dressed, well-organized, relaxed and prepared sales representative is vastly superior to a rushed, disheveled, disorganized person. If you are late without a valid excuse, it might be assumed that your product will be late or incomplete. You do indeed reflect the product or service you represent. You benefit from being on time, and your sales improve. Start earlier, try to arrive earlier, and chart the improvement.

If you have a real problem with this, you should then do some serious troubleshooting to determine the causes of your problem. If you need to do more to prepare the evening before, then that should be done. Being on time demonstrates a respect for your customer's time and for your own time. This is another area where you can get a step up on the competition and secure more business. Be on time all the time—it's worth the extra effort.

THOROUGHNESS: PAYING ATTENTION TO DETAILS

As a salesperson, virtually everything you do is a reflection of the quality of your product. One of the most critical factors in sales is your attention to detail. It could be the mathematical computation of the price, spelling on any written document, or memory of your customer's situation. If you are careless or sloppy in your work, many negative consequences can ensue. Assumptions might be made about your level of professionalism. A salesperson who has many positive qualities (pleasant appearance, promptness, friendliness) can lose sales because of the inability to attend to details. Be sure to dot the *i*'s, cross the *t*'s, and don't neglect the decimal points and fine print. Know your business backward, forward, and inside out. Proofread, double-check, and take your time with the details.

A seemingly minor detail can set you apart from your competitors. Some customers are forgiving of our errors if they have a positive past history with us. But new or prospective customers are often supersensitive to minor errors that could predict future disasters. Will you send them the correct quantity, color, size, crew at the agreed-upon time? Focus on all of the critical facts. Don't leave any stone unturned to secure and maintain business. Also, it helps to be rested when you are writing orders so that you minimize the fatigue factor, a common culprit in the cause of errors and oversights.

How do we improve our attention to detail? One way is by not overloading our minds with impertinent facts. Another is to take legible and detailed notes during meetings. Then, review and revise those notes and communicate to the customer the facts that seem to matter to him. Don't be in a hurry—take your time. Double-check your briefcase to make certain you have your samples and brochures. Always have business cards with you. Check your pockets/purse to be certain you have your wallet prior to a lunch or dinner engagement.

Customers are impressed when we remember birthdays, birthplaces, hobbies, or the activities of their children. Seemingly minor facts can mean major points scored. Concentrate carefully on what is being said and on what you see.

Verbalize facts to yourself to fix them in your memory. Make a quick review sheet if necessary so that you will remember things. Sometimes you have only one opportunity to close a sale, and it completely depends upon your attention to detail. Be sure-handed and sure-minded with your business matters. Focus on the details, and you will be amply rewarded.

PROFILE 3—Terry Guinn
Attention to Detail

Terry Guinn sells electronic and exhibit moving. His customers relocate electronic equipment and convention displays and exhibits. He has produced in excess of $1 million for each of the past six years. In 1986 he produced $2 million, and was the top producing Mayflower salesman in his category. Terry's forte is thoroughness and attention to detail. He has secured and maintained high volume accounts primarily because of that factor.

Terry is basically a soft-spoken man of forty years. He is not really dynamic or charismatic. In fact, he doesn't even aggressively call on new accounts. But he is a master at delving deeply into the inner workings of the accounts he does have. He takes care of his accounts, which in turn generates more business. His approach is definitely quality over quantity.

Prior to securing an account, he does extensive research about the company so that he can speak intelligently about the type of product he will be shipping. He then puts together highly detailed proposals that are price-competitive. His product knowledge is very high, which assists him in his proposal writing. He knows what he's talking about.

Terry has developed a strong working relationship with Mayflower corporate offices. This relationship becomes important when he has an account or order that requires special needs. His knowledge of the intricate details of the service he provides makes him a valuable ally to his accounts. He continues to monitor the service long after he has secured the business.

His attention to detail is particularly appropriate for the type of business he solicits. In the shipment of sensitive equipment, buyers are concerned with the details of how and when machines are shipped. They appreciate the fact that Terry is an expert who is apprised of all of the pertinent details of his job.

BECOMING A SELF-STARTER: STAYING ACTIVE

The major difference between sales and other careers is that, in sales, you must become a self-starter. In many sales positions, you are allowed as much freedom as you desire if you are a producer. Some sales managers place heavy restrictions upon their trainees by requiring a certain number of calls to be made, and not demanding that they be self-starters during the training period. But once they are cut loose, they must learn to motivate themselves and become active and productive in a hurry.

What does this mean for you in practical terms? First of all, YOU ARE REALLY YOUR OWN BOSS. In fact, salespeople who fail to grasp this fact rarely succeed in sales. Your sales manager might be your direct supervisor, but it is you who must get yourself out of bed and out into the field. You might be able to fool other people when you are slacking off in your work, but you can't fool yourself.

A self-starter likes the independence of a sales career, but does not abuse it. I personally thrive on the schedule freedom that sales allows me. I can make my own schedule within certain limits. If I were to abuse this privilege habitually by playing instead of working, it would show in my sales results. On the other hand, once you have begun to establish yourself, you should take advantage of being in sales by enjoying some of the flexibility that it provides in your schedule.

An effective self-starter stays active by engaging in a variety of tasks throughout the day. If you have cold called for three hours, you might take a break, after which you could go back into the office and return phone calls or organize your leads. During a lull you might call a lead source to generate some new leads and get yourself motivated.

If you are not a self-starter by nature, then sales might not be the ideal career for you. However, not all successful salespeople are natural self-starters. In fact, once you get established in sales, there is less of a need to be a self-starter due to the volume of business that you have already generated and now must attend to. The difficulty arises at the early stages of your career when you have no established business. If your sales manager provides enough structure in the beginning, then your lack of initiative might not hurt your performance. It should be noted at this point that I strongly disagree with sales managers who continue to demand that salespeople stay in the office unnecessarily or at times when they should be out in the field. One well-known phone company requires that all salespeople report to the office every day at 8:30 a.m. and again at 4:30 p.m. The major problem with this is that it cuts into what might be prime selling time for certain customers.

Another method that can help you in this area of self-starting is to set a very tight schedule for yourself. If you do so, it will force you to work hard and consistently. The danger of doing this is to not allow sufficient time between appointments. Scheduling in itself can be difficult in that you don't usually know exactly how long a given meeting or appointment will take, or if the customer might cancel a meeting without having the courtesy to call you.

If you have problems getting started or staying motivated, there are several things you can do, including the following:

1. Schedule breakfast meetings.

2. Schedule early morning appointments.

3. Go into the office early every day until the habit of getting an early start is established.

Never forget that your performance is directly related to your effort and ability. Change your habits if necessary in order to get going in the morning. Set as many appointments as you can effectively handle until you get into the habit of working full days on your own without being told to do so. Once the new patterns are established, you are on your way to an enjoyable career that allows you adequate free time.

MANAGING YOUR TIME

The amount of potential free time that salespeople have is sometimes a source of anxiety. How do we go about managing our time to achieve maximal productivity? Part of the answer to this question depends on your motivational level. However, regardless of your goals, you need to learn to manage your time effectively.

You should begin by seeing time in terms of quality rather than quantity. That is, don't focus on how long you work in a given day. You should focus more upon what you accomplish—that is, your RESULTS. One of the main advantages of sales is that you can successfully work your own hours once you reach a certain level of competence and productivity.

In becoming aware of yourself, you should know whether you are more of a "morning person" or not. If you are, then you might get the majority of your work done before noon. If not, then you might not even get into full gear before noon. Depending on the nature of your product/service, it might be necesssary to modify your patterns of waking and sleeping. If you are a morning type but your potential customers are not, then you need to adjust your normal schedule.

One major reason that people have difficulty managing their time is that they waste time. Some wasted time is expected for everyone. But you need to become focused during prime selling hours to sell. People or situations that interfere with selling must be given a lower priority. There are several types of things that should be done during non-peak hours or to fill some of the "dead time" between appointments:

1. Getting fuel for your car

2. Washing your car

3. Going to the cleaners

4. Having your shoes shined

5. Paperwork

You can begin the process of better time management by first analyzing how you currently spend and waste time. Then you can develop a plan for utilizing your time better. Ultimately *you* are the one who determines when and how you do things. Your sales manager, wife, or friends might make certain suggestions or demands, but none of them knows the total picture of your schedule. Sometimes people will try to monopolize your time. You need to be able to discipline yourself in these cases.

A major part of using time is momentum. There are times when we are operating at maximal efficiency, truly "on a roll." When this is happening, it is important not to let other things disrupt this flow. Even if we had planned to stop at a certain time, our momentum should be maintained as long as our energy level remains high. The reverse of this is also true. When we can't get going, sometimes it is better to take a break than to force the work. Often, when we come back to the task we are in a better frame of mind to be productive.

The bottom line here is productivity. In commission sales, you are paid for results, not for the amount of time you spend on the job. Your level of success is a direct result of your efficient use of time. People new to sales often have difficulties because they still see their job as being one with fixed hours. If you need twelve-hour days to finish all of your tasks, then work twelve hours. But if you can complete everything to your satisfaction in eight hours, then there is no reason to feel guilty. The focus is on RESULTS. It is your time, so learn to use it wisely.

PLANNING AND SALES STRATEGIES

Selling is not a random, spontaneous activity. To be effective, you need to plan your activities. This can be done on a daily, weekly, and monthly basis. The important thing is to develop a workable plan prior to the beginning of each period (be it day, week, month, or year). Your calendar will tell you what is scheduled, and should be reviewed frequently. This is all part of being organized.

Any plan is subject to change, and it is necessary for you to be flexible. If a two-hour meeting is cancelled, you should be able to fill that time with some productive alternative. Along with planning, you need to develop ongoing sales strategies. These might be strategies for securing specific business or general strategies for how you will spend your time and effort.

Highly successful salespeople have goals, and specific plans to attain those goals. The plans should always have alternatives, in the event that certain aspects fail. If Plan A doesn't work, then you can proceed to Plans B and C.

I ponder my sales strategy constantly. I do this primarily during driving time or on my daily walks. It's fun for me to consider the various alternatives and which ones I'm going to choose. I attribute much of my success to this cerebral activity. In fact, this is one of my favorite parts of selling.

Sales can be a very loosely structured activity. Because of this, you need to bring some order to it through strategic planning. You can use your insight and creativity to determine the appropriate time for specific activities. You are the master of your own destiny. Consider your moves carefully, and act decisively.

PART II

CONTACT WITH POTENTIAL CUSTOMERS

6

FOR OPENERS:
A COLD-CALLING SYSTEM
THAT WORKS!

Prospecting or cold calling is the lifeblood of sales. Without a consistent effort, high levels of success cannot be achieved. The primary purpose of cold calling is to generate leads for potential customers. Another important reason is to find out who the decision makers are at various companies. Cold calling generates new business. There are three major cold calls approaches: via the phone, in person or by the mail. This section will discuss each of those mediums.

The telephone allows a salesperson to make numerous calls in a large geographic area without leaving the office. Time can be saved by calling rather than visiting certain potential clients. It should be noted that the primary purpose of using the phone in prospecting is to schedule appointments, which then lead to sales. The phone is also utilized to qualify and screen out customers who offer no potential or very low potential for business.

In my personal calling system I write down calls made, and maintain a continually updated and revised call back schedule. I prioritize the importance of various calls by date. By doing this, I am assured of getting to the high priority or timely customer on time. There are several software programs specifically designed for systematizing the telemarketing process. Some of the more popular ones are Instant Recall, Telemagic, and ACT. A central principle of successful selling is to make timely calls on clients over a period of time in order to secure business.

In the transportation industry, specifically commercial office moving, there is a certain time "window" that customers typically contact movers for cost proposals/bids. For example, I might have been scheduled to call back Joe Banks on June 1, but he calls me on May 23 to schedule an appointment. My call back system has me call on a regular basis, in case the customer doesn't call me. I never rely on a potential customer calling me back. This note of caution should be heeded. You will not reach high levels of success if you wait for the phone to ring. Don't pester potential customers, but keep in touch. It is helpful to ask them directly how often they would like you to call on them to solicit their business. Most potential clients will provide you with some guidance, by suggesting weekly, monthly or some other time frame for future calls.

We are not always in the mood or proper frame of mind to cold call. I tend to work in very intense spurts, when I can make numerous calls during a short period of time. Cold calling is not intended to replace or take priority over sales presentations or critical administrative matters. But if you have completed your previously required paperwork, then it is time to cold call.

Why and when is cold calling in person effective? First of all, it is important to understand what is is you can accomplish in person that you can't do over the phone or through the mail. By physically calling, you are likely to discover potential business that you could not get any other way. You might also be able to meet potential customers and even conduct business. I use physical cold calling periodically at this stage in my career. I almost always uncover something new during a cold calling expedition. I perceive it as a kind of treasure hunt or detective outing. Perhaps the most important reason for cold calling in person is the inherent advantage of face-to-face communication. People tend to treat you differently when you are a real live person standing in front of them rather than a voice on the phone or a letter in the mail.

The mail has several valuable functions, quite different from either the phone or in-person visits. A pre-call letter prepares the customer for your call. Pre-call letters are especially effective with busy people, and they mark you as a professional. Other types of mail can serve the purpose of keeping your name, company, and product/service in front of the customer. Most people want something "in writing" at some point. You can be very creative in terms of what you send them and when you send it to them.

These three channels (phone, in person, mail) should all be utilized in concert with one another. A balanced approach will serve the general purpose of getting you in the door and moving toward business. The highest achieving salespeople are usually strong in at least two of these areas.

The specific procedure that I have refined over several years is as follows:

1. I secure a lead that a company is moving to a new facility.

2. I call the company and ask for the person who is responsible for coordinating the relocation.

3. If that person is available, I ask if they are accepting moving proposals at that time. If the answer is affirmative, I immediately try to set up an appointment. If the answer is negative, I inquire as to when this process is likely to commence. When given the answer, I offer to send some literature and determine when I should next call back. The literature allows them to familiarize themselves with my company and call me back.

4. If the person is not available, I continue to call until I reach him or her. Then proceed with Step 3. Step 3 might have to be repeated over several months or longer before an appointment can be scheduled.

It is important to keep calling on a regular basis. In most cases, the decision maker is happy to have the salesperson call. However, try to determine an appropriate time period that keeps your name in front of the customer. Over a period of months, a rapport is likely to develop. By the time a formal meeting is scheduled, it is no longer a "cold call."

A positive attitude is vital to effective cold calling. You cannot be overly fearful of rejection. It is part of the business. It is not *you* who is being rejected, so don't take it personally. Be an actor, make a game of it. Have fun. After a while, you will have regular times for cold calling. You will strike a positive balance between new and old business. Call, call, call and you will sell, sell, sell.

PROFILE 4—Bill Saleebey
Relentless Cold Calling

Perhaps more than any single factor, my relentless cold calling has been responsible for my success in sales. When I first started, I was a bit timid about cold calling. In retrospect, I think it was because I lacked the knowledge and confidence in what I was doing. As I learned more about my business, I began to increase my volume of cold calling. My primary modes of cold calling were in person and on the phone.

By cold calling in person, I would continually uncover new sources of business. Not only would I generate bona fide leads, but I would invariably get some new ideas about possible business. There is really no substitute for in-person cold calling. You can do much on the phone, but by calling in person, you open up doors that you might never have discovered. Phone calling would allow me to set appointments and make contact with potential customers in a wide geographic area. Often I would spend one day in the field and the next day calling those individuals whose business cards or names I had gotten while in the field. My goal in phone calling was primarily to set appointments. If I couldn't get an appointment, I would determine the time for my next call.

Cold calling provides me with a constant bank of potential business. By continuing to cold call even after I had reached high levels of productivity, I was able to assure myself of a stable income. Cold calling plants the seeds for future business. It can be fun and exciting. As long as you're able to take rejection with a good attitude, you'll find that cold calling will make your job much more fulfilling and profitable.

Perhaps my greatest single sales success story to date is that of a company called Teradata. It began with a cold call in which I merely left my business card. Shortly after doing so, I read in a local newspaper that Teradata happened to be the fastest growing company in Los Angeles. About two weeks after leaving my card, I placed a phone call to the decision maker. He called back in a week and gave me an order. We did an excellent job and became Teradata's regular office movers. It came to pass that this fast-growing company was running out of space and needed to relocate approximately a thousand employees to a new headquarters. In competitive bidding, I was awarded the contract for that relocation. So, from a little seed, a giant tree grew. Cold calling pays off.

PERSISTENCE

It has been said that the sales process truly begins with the initial rejection or negative response. If sales were an easy career to succeed in, then many more people would be doing it. The fact is that few salespeople do not face rejection at one time or another. I have never met a salesperson with a perfect closing ratio. Thus, virtually every person who has ever sold anything has had to face some rejection. There have been many documented cases of individuals, who were initially overwhelmed by rejection, going on to phenomenal sales careers. Therefore, we must learn how to go beyond the initial phase of rejection and continue to try until we achieve success.

We can accomplish this by persistence. In short, we do not take *no* for an answer. The prospective customer is saying no now. Our job is to change that *no* to a *yes*. Persistence does not mean that we do not respect the buyer's decision. Rather, we need to put more effort into persuading that person that they should give us their business. Persistence does not mean that you badger people or are rude to them. My definition of persistence is a professional, polite practice of not giving up merely because a person says no to us initially. We can do this in several ways, depending upon the nature of the rejection. Some of the ways are:

1. Try to answer objections to the satisifaction of the customer.

2. Be willing to make some concessions or to negotiate in order to close a sale.

3. Politely ask if there is any chance that you can get an opportunity to secure even a small order.

4. Continue to call on accounts in a variety of creative ways.

5. Send samples of your product in order to arouse interest and to get an order.

People have many different styles of persistence. My bias is strongly toward a nonaggressive approach. People tend to resist more vigorously when they feel they are being pressured too hard or manipulated. Stay in there. Keep trying to secure the business. But, if you are getting strong signals to back off, do so. Don't quit, but give the buyer some breathing room. Then, after a reasonable delay, try again, and if necessary, again. Success comes to those who are persistent.

Profile 5—Layne Middleton
Persistence and Taking Care of Accounts

Layne Middleton is a forty-year-old woman who sells magazine advertising space. She is attractive, articulate, and highly professional. She has been in sales for only three years, and has already established new sales records for her territory. Layne has had no formal sales training. What factors have led to her success?

First of all, she has several years of prior experience in the advertising profession. This fact gave her immediate product knowledge. Second, she is a hard worker who always gives her best effort and a full day's work. She is intelligent, grasps the major components of her work, and knows what it takes to sell ads. But her major asset is *persistence*. She is driven to land accounts, especially difficult ones. She meets an initial *no* answer with a determined attitude of changing it into a *yes*. She tries creative ways to get the business. It seems as though she gets energized by the more difficult challenges. Without being pushy, she will come back to prospective customers with different ideas to secure their business.

Once she gets the account, her second cardinal trait enters the picture: she takes care of the account. This involves regular contact, entertainment, and making sure that the ad is correct. The client is treated as a treasured friend or member of her family. This personal attention insures loyalty and continued business. Layne makes the client feel that she will always do whatever she can to make certain that the ads are correct and that they generate new business.

EXCHANGING BUSINESS LEADS

In many sales careers, it is beneficial to exchange leads with individuals in related fields. This type of networking can produce numerous leads for all parties involved. The best approach in exchanging leads is to start out by *giving* rather than asking for leads. Be generous but cautious. It is usually better to deal with individuals who only exchange leads with one person in each field. I refuse to exchange leads with someone who, in turn, exchanges leads with other people in my industry. The danger here is that the person will take all of your leads and pass them along to a competitor.

The best lead-exchanging situations are fairly equal. But don't be concerned if one person gives more at certain points in time. Lead exchanges can develop into referral exchanges if trust develops to a sufficient level. In my business, for example, the best sources for lead exchanges are: business phone salespeople, furniture refinishers, commercial real estate brokers, space planners, and building managers. I have built relationships with several commercial real estate brokers who regularly send me lists of companies who are planning to relocate, providing me with potential customers.

Use your imagination. Sometimes there is a gold mine just waiting to be tapped by you. Communication and trust are the keys in exchanging leads. The more you give, the more you get. One of my lead sources began with me giving massive numbers of leads for about a year and my getting little in return. But those gestures were not forgotten. Now I get about ten leads per week from that person. If you carefully develop and cultivate a cadre of lead sources, your well will never run dry. Stay in touch with your lead sources, and try to help them in any way you can. Take care of your people, and they will take care of you.

NETWORKING

Networking has become one of the major buzzwords of our time. And for good reason. Effective networking can lead to a tremendous business base. What is networking? Essentially, it is the exchange of business information and services through a group of associated individuals, meeting in groups or on an individual basis. For example, I have a group of friends, acquaintances, and business associates. One of my friends needs a refrigerator. A business associate sells refrigerators. So I put them in touch with one another, with me as the nexus or connector. Chambers of commerce often have monthly mixers where people can openly network. Truly effective networking involves a careful cataloguing of who does what for whom and where. That is, I can put Joe the chiropractor from Pasadena in touch with moving companies or insurance companies in the Pasadena area.

The essence of networking is communication and the desire to help others, and expand an endeavor or business. You must have a realistic motivation to go out of your way to help others.

It is through the mutually generous give-and-take that networking derives its power. But you must be willing to give and share rather than just reaping the benefits. Talk to as many people as you can about what you do. In turn, ask others about their friends, careers, and interests. An added dimension of networking is that you not only receive assistance from your sources, but you get information from people they know. Thus, your business possibilities are expanded substantially through networking. Get out into the world, and find out what is happening.

HONESTY IS THE
ONLY POLICY
The TRUTH Brings
Solid Results

It is unfortunate, but true, that the term *salesman* is not usually associated with honesty. In fact, it might be said that there is a widespread stereotype portraying salesmen as sneaky, sweet-smelling, slick, aggressive creeps in polyester suits and fake gold jewelry. These overbearing slobs are constantly trying to come between us and our money. And frankly, there have been many salesmen over the years who reinforce this notion.

Why do people not tell the truth? Primarily, it's because they believe the truth will either cause them problems or jeopardize a sale. They are uncomfortable about being honest. The fact is that lies and distortions cause many more problems than the truth ever did. Customers want to know what is really happening. They're more comfortable with the truth in the long run. They want honest answers to some of the following questions: How long will the product last? Is it designed for its intended purpose? Why was the shipment late or incorrect?

What guarantees are applicable? Am I getting a fair price? What is the level of quality? What role will you take if problems come up? What happened? What is this particular charge for?

Honesty applies both to the product/service and the salesperson's performance. One veteran sales success, when asked about the most critical aspects of selling, stated flatly, "Admit it when you make a mistake and it will save you much grief." Beginners often mistakenly try to hide their errors. But there is a clear benefit in the long run to own up honestly to our errors, omissions, tardiness, or our company's mistakes or poor performance. We might lose face momentarily, but honesty signals integrity, which is the cornerstone of effective selling.

Sometimes an honest answer to a prospective customer's question might cause you to lose a sale. But the honesty may gain you respect. In addition, if you are not honest, you might spend more time and energy in the long run trying to recover from your initial distortion. For example, instead of admitting a mistake or oversight, you can waste valuable time and energy trying to cover up the problem. You must resist the temptation to lie, because the lies will come back to haunt you. Honesty will generate the type of business that you are best equipped to service properly.

THE IMPORTANCE OF INTEGRITY

Integrity refers to an adherence to a set of values. In sales, it means a consistent and abiding honesty and genuine concern for the well-being of our customer. Integrity is something that is earned rather than assumed. It goes beyond honesty. When you have integrity you express on a regular basis as much concern for your customers as you might for a friend or family member. Your word can be trusted without any doubt.

When you are perceived to have integrity, your business will grow by leaps and bounds. People place their trust in you and your decisions. Often, customers will let you decide how much of your product they need. You have moved far beyond the peddler that some people consider a salesperson.

PROFILE 6—Jeff Miller
Warmth, Honesty, Integrity

Jeff Miller sells toys to major department stores. He is sixty years old and has been in the wholesale toy business for over twenty-five years. He has written over $5 million per year in business for the past fifteen years. What is it that makes him successful? It is, of course, a combination of many things. He has very strong product knowledge, believes in his company (his brother is the owner), and is a good communicator. But what makes him special is his warm, sincere personality.

Jeff truly cares about the personal lives of his customers. He is a compassionate human being before anything else. His honesty and integrity are exemplary. In his business, the customer must take much on faith. He will come into their store and virtually tell them what they need, how much they need, and will present them with new products that he believes will sell in their stores. I have witnessed him entering a store, going through the toy department, and writing up an entire order on his own. Because of the level of trust that he has established, he then gets the signature and begins to socialize with the customer. A beginning salesperson could not take that kind of liberty.

In order to reach that point with a customer, Jeff has to build a high level of trust. He does this by getting to know his customers on a personal basis. This includes meeting their families and remembering names, birthdays, and pertinent facts. His warmth is contagious; one feels very comfortable around him. He will never sell you something you don't need merely to make an extra commission. If a particular item doesn't sell, he will take it back without a question. If he makes a mistake, he will admit it immediately. If there is any problem, he makes certain that it is rectified promptly. In sum, he takes care of his customers and induces a loyalty in them that leads to long-term and prosperous accounts.

8

PRODUCT KNOWLEDGE THE KEY TO CREDIBILITY

Two major reasons that people buy from a particular salesperson are confidence and trust in him or her. When I go into a clothing store to buy a new suit, I'm looking for a salesperson who knows about clothes: fabric, style, color and value. I want to do business with an expert. Most beginning salespeople lose sales for one major reason: insufficient product knowledge. They simply don't know what they are doing.

It takes time and considerable effort to become an expert in your chosen field. Knowing about the benefits of your product/service is necessary, but nor sufficient. You must be able to communicate this knowledge clearly and effectively. The successful sales person glows with knowledge and confidence. They leave no doubt in the prospective customer's mind about their product/service. The knowledge should be communicated concisely and enthusiastically. The information should be relevant to the expressed needs of the buyer. Buyers are concerned with themselves, not the "general public." Men are interested in men's clothing, not theories of fashion design. Although a salesperson might possess a vast reservoir of knowledge, not all of it is useful for every presentation. The professional knows how to highlight the important points and briefly summarize minor points.

In making a sales presentation, it is essential to summarize the benefits of your particular product/service. Use relevant examples to illustrate your points. Don't assume that the customer knows anything unless you have prior knowledge that they do. Present your information in such a way that it makes your client comfortable in selecting you. Your job is very basic—to convince people beyond a shadow of a doubt to buy from you. When you have closed a sale, then it is vital to ensure that they receive exactly what you have promised them. Good salespeople can sell. Exceptional salespeople generate multiple sales, repeat business and referrals.

Product knowledge is communicated in both obvious and subtle ways from the moment you first encounter the prospective customer. You know what to look for, you zero in on critical points, and can answer many questions without ever referring to any literature or "cheat sheets." The following list gives examples of what you should know.

1. Do you know what products and services your company has available?

2. Do you know prices and rates by heart, or do you have to look them up?

3. Are you familiar with trade jargon and terminology?

4. Can you answer questions that are posed to you in a reasonable period of time?

5. Are you attentive to relevant details regarding the sale?

6. Do you focus too much on the sales process and not enough on the customer's needs?

7. Can you solve problems or obstacles that arise during and after the sale?

The importance of product knowledge cannot be overemphasized. Quite simply, people buy from people who know what they are doing. Every effort should be made to project the image of a professional salesperson who is completely familiar with every major aspect of the product/service you represent. Don't downplay or minimize your role. You are the expert. Your primary goal should be to do everything in your power to assist the customer in achieving superior quality service. If you don't know something, admit it. And then learn about it. Study, ask questions, take courses if necessary, and gain command of your domain. Without knowledge, there will be no excellence. Learn it, communicate it, and sell it.

PROFILE 7—Jeff Nichols
Product Knowledge

Jeff was the first salesperson I trained. He came into sales straight "off the trucks," where he had worked for eight years as a mover and foreman. He knew the moving business very well from an operational standpoint. in short, he entered sales with a high level of product knowledge. He still needed to learn to translate this knowledge into a sales perspective, but he knew the basics.

Jeff began in sales at age thirty. He attended college in Southern California, where he is a few units short of a Bachelor's degree. He played college and semi-pro baseball. As a truckman, he was able to earn in excess of $50,000 per year for several years immediately prior to entering sales. In addition to having a knowledge of the moving industry in general, his experience was with our company in particular. Therefore, he was familiar with many of the same policies and procedures that would apply to sales. Jeff is of average height and build, trim and athletic. I would describe his appearance as pleasant, cheerful, and honest. He is softspoken, fairly even-tempered, and very likable.

Jeff had no previous sales training prior to working with me. His level of self-confidence was not particularly high in terms of selling. But what he had as a major strength was his detailed knowledge of the moving business. This knowledge contributed heavily to the development of his self-confidence and his ultimate belief that he could be successful in sales. Simply stated, he knew what he was talking about, and it showed. People believed in him because he knew what it took and what it cost to perform a move. What he lacked in formal sales techniques he more than compensated for with an in-depth product/service knowledge.

His first year's performance earned him Rookie of the Year honors. in his second full year of selling, he was presented with the award for highest percentage over quota, and sold more than $500,000 in moving. This is a fantastic achievement for a person who had never sold a thing prior to beginning with our company. i would attribute most of Jeff's success to his product knowledge and his ability to communicate it in an honest and forthright manner.

EXERCISE 7—Increasing Product Knowledge

How much do you know about the product/service you represent? This exercise is designed to assesss your current level of product knowledge and to increase it.

List the major features of your primary product/service.

Expand upon each feature by demonstrating the major benefits derived from each.

Make a list of the major aspects of your product/ service in which you lack sufficient knowledge.

- How can you increase your product knowledge in each area?

- What do you plan to do to increase your product knowledge in weak areas?

- Can you take any classes, read any books or manuals, or learn from an individual?

You will not reach your potential until you increase your product knowledge. Begin taking notes if you don't already do so to broaden your base of information. if necessary, memorize some of the major benefits of your product/service. As you product knowledge increases, so will your sales.

9

ASKING
THE RIGHT QUESTIONS
LISTENING CAREFULLY
TO THE ANSWERS

B efore you try to sell anything, you must determine what is important to the buyer. This is done primarily by systematic questioning. For example, when you walk into a shoe store, the salesperson should find out what type of shoe you are shopping for before trying to sell you anything. Inexperienced salespeople often try to sell something before they even know what the buyer wants. Don't skip this vital step in the sales process. Without it, you will not get far with most customers. Done effectively, it can often generate much more business than you imagined. For example, in the moving and storage business, I could sell the following: office moving, household goods moving, electronic moving, trade shows, international moving, record storage and new product shipping. Although I specialize in office moving, questioning can lead to other types of business. Questions can be asked about specific matters or general topics. The questioning period is often an ideal time to develop rapport by asking such things as:

- ❖ Do you live around here?

- ❖ Where do your children go to school?

- ❖ Have you been in the new shopping mall yet?

However, the major reason for asking questions is to focus on what the buyer wants, needs, and is concerned about. Some of the most common topics are:

- ❖ Price—this includes discounting, overtime rates, and the differences between estimates and actual final costs.

- ❖ Quality of Product/Service—this topic requires some evidence from the salesperson.

- ❖ Reputation of your company.

- ❖ Timeliness—"when do you need to receive the product?"

- ❖ References.

- ❖ Your involvement in the transaction—here the buyer might ask you to be present during the job or to review the invoice in detail after the completion of the project.

- ❖ Your experience.

- ❖ Prestige.

- ❖ Name (Mayflower, Cadillac, Rolex, Brooks Brothers).

- ❖ Guarantees.

Before launching into your sales presentation, you need to determine the criteria being used for the buying decision. Otherwise, you might give a brilliant presentation about matters that mean little or nothing to the customer. The questions can be phrased in several ways. Some examples are:

1. What concerns you about ...?

2. What are you going to base your decision on?

3. What criteria are you using to select ...?

4. What's important to you?

5. Are there any specific problem areas that I should know about?

Your primary goal here is to find out what is really motivating the buyer. You also want to find out how much the buyer knows about your product/service. Don't assume too much. Are they well informed or naive? Sometimes they will tell you up front about their level of expertise. How much experience do they have with your product/service or that of your competitor? When you get answers to your questions, listen attentively and *take notes*. Eventually you will develop a written proposal and sales presentation that addresses these issues. If price is not mentioned by the buyer, then you probably shouldn't focus too much on price. If references are mentioned as an important factor, then you need to take care to provide current, relevant references, and to highlight them in the sales presentation. Reference letters are particularly effective. Encourage the buyer to check your references.

By asking appropriate questions, you focus in on the buyer's motives. You then sell based on issues that are important to the buyer, not to you. Even if your company has a wonderful new feature, it should not be emphasized if the buyer expresses a total lack of interest in it. You need to continually vary your approach to questioning in response to the different types of buyers. For example, some customers will give brief answers, and you will reach the end of your "list" in a hurry. You will sometimes have potential questions answered before you have the opportunity to ask them. Have a basic plan for questioning. But, be continually open to changing your format due to circumstances. In addition, you might benefit by asking for elaboration or further explanations to certain answers. Thus, a strictly memorized series of standard questions can be counterproductive, and this method should be avoided.

There is yet another basic function of asking questions. Good questions make you appear professional. They can actually take the pressure and spotlight off of you and allow you to assess the situation. Whereas novice salespeople often don't know which questions to ask, professionals do their "homework" before they try to sell anything. Answers to the questions then provide tools to sell our product. Ask, listen, write, use the answers and make more sales.

LISTENING SKILLS: DEVELOPING EMPATHY AND SENSITIVITY

One of the keys to sales success is the ability to listen carefully to what the customer is saying. You must hear exactly what is being said, and also know what might be behind those words. Listening attentively, determining possible hidden meanings, and remembering what you learn can make you more effective. It means a lot to a person to be *really* heard and understood. Too many salespeople are so concerned with making a sale that they forget to stay tuned into the needs of the customer.

From the moment you first encounter the customer, you will be told many things. Some of them are more important than others. You should make a habit of writing down key points and maintaining a file for each customer. Listening skills can be developed through practice. In order to listen effectively, you must tone down your own talking and energy level. It helps to repeat certain statements made by the customer, not only for clarification but also to assist your memory. This *mirroring* or *reflection of feeling* helps to let the customer know you really hear *and* understand what is being said.

Empathy is the ability to accurately identify with the world and situation of others. When you develop empathy, you can then become more aware of the concerns and feelings of the customer. This empathy should flow from a genuine concern for the welfare of the customer.

For example, let's say that a customer communicates to you that if a particular order is incorrect, his job is in jeopardy. That means that the customer's job is dependent upon the accuracy of your work. In a case like this, you can communicate to the customer that you take this fact very seriously. You could make a comment like this: "Joe, I realize how important this project is to you, and that your job depends on it. I will personally assure you that it will be done correctly. If there are any problems at all, I will discuss them with your supervisor. I don't want you to lose your job. I know how important it is to you."

Listening involves prioritizing certain statements made by the customer over others. Sometimes the customer will specifically state that you should remember something in particular. In other cases, it is the repetition of a statement that underscores its importance. You need to be sensitive to critical buying motives, concerns, and other things that are important to the buyer. These can relate to time, cost, special situations, or other factors.

Good listening skills are one of the most important components of successful selling. You must know what is important to the buyer at every stage of the selling process. If you are uncertain about something, clarify it. Ask specific questions about what is important to the customer. If you have forgotten something, it is usually better to ask about it than to assume you will remember. Pay attention to details. They may mean the difference between making and losing a sale.

PROFILE 8—Charlene Rose
Questions Before Action

Charlene Rose sells business phones on a national account basis. Her approach to sales emphasizes the systematic use of questions prior to any selling. She takes the potential customer through a series of questions designed to elicit the following:

1. Needs

2. Concerns

3. Buying motives

4. Problems with previous vendors (if relevant)

5. Volume of business

6. Billing procedures

7. Expectations of account manager

She has managed to secure many major accounts through her methods. Her bookings have exceeded $1 million annually for over ten years. The key to her method is to find out exactly what the client wants and needs prior to preparing a proposal. She never presents generic proposals. Each one is specially tailored to the client in response to the questions she asks.

Of course, she has other attributes and skills. She is pleasant looking, dresses well, is articulate and friendly. She knows the telecommunications business inside and out. This combination of skills allows her to compete successfully for major national accounts. But her major skill is that of asking the appropriate questions, listening carefully to the answers, and incorporating those answers into her sales presentation.

EXERCISE 8—Asking Questions

How do you begin a sale? Do you start with a question or a statement? It is useful to begin your encounter with your customer by asking questions to determine basic needs. In this exercise, begin by listing all of the questions that you might use in an initial meeting.

After you have done this, rank the questions in order of priority. Why are certain questions more important than others? Are you comfortable working from a set list of questions? What are the main reasons for asking the customer questions? What use should you make of the answers given by the customer? Use your imagination. Good questions will lead you in the right direction, toward the sale.

10

QUALITY ANd QUANTITY
of AppoiNTMENTS
STrikiNq THE
PERFECT BALANCE
TO MAKE ENDS MEET

S uccessful salespeople make many sales calls in order to generate business. At the same time, they learn not to rush customers in an effort to reach certain sales levels. They make a large quantity of quality calls. How is this possible? At first, there will probably be an emphasis on quantity. This was true in my own case. I really didn't know any better at the time. Only after I clearly realized that I was losing sales because of haste and lack of thoroughness did I begin to emphasize quality. Today, my focus is much more upon quality. However, my numbers have remained high due to consistent effort and prospecting.

What does this mean in practice? First of all, salespeople must make a certain number of sales calls in order to make sufficient commissions to earn a living. The better the closing ratio, the fewer calls needed. The issue of quality enters into the picture at this point. When do I cut off a potential customer if it is almost certain that I have (or haven't) made a sale? How much time should I spend with a customer? When is "small talk" a waste of time, an excuse not to work, or, on the contrary, a valuable opportunity to deepen the rapport? These questions must be answered on an individual basis. Experience will help you to find the most effective answers for each circumstance.

Successful salespeople seem to sense intuitively the amount and quality of time to be spent with a particular client. They are selective about prospects, and have learned from experience to read the signals that influence those decisions. For example, let's assume it is 2:45 and you have already spent forty-five minutes with a customer. The customer, seemingly insensitive to your waning interest level and schedule, is literally rambling on about a topic in which you have no interest. You have a 3:00 appointment which you consider vitally important. You are ten minutes away from that meeting place. What would you do? One possibility is to be polite to the "rambler," ignoring your next appointment. Another is to abruptly say, "I've gotta go," stand up, and begin heading toward the door. Perhaps the best response is to tactfully terminate the monologue and hurry (while not appearing to be rude) to your next meeting. The exact reaction depends upon several factors, such as:

1. The nature of the rambling

2. The relative importance of each meeting

3. How the rambler might interpret your response

4. The possible consequences of each response

Numerous situations arise that test a salesperson's ability to decide the length of meetings or calls. We must regularly choose how long to spend with a particular customer. These decisions can have major consequences for our sales results. Some of the questions to be considered, either prior to or during a meeting, are:

1. How busy is the prospective customer?

2. How complicated is the sale?

3. How much is the sale worth?

4. Who wants to prolong or hasten the call, you or the customer?

5. How busy are you?

6. How motivated are you?

7. When is it appropriate to terminate a meeting or call?

8. How should a meeting/call be terminated?

What I most want to emphasize here is that quality calls are necessary for sales success. We must be continually vigilant against the tendency to rush clients—without, however, allowing our time to be dominated by certain low-probability prospects. We live in a highly stressful, often impersonal, fast-paced society. People usually welcome the chance to slow down for a moment and make real human contact. I have seen many salespeople close deals simply because they took more time and care with a customer than the competition. Make many calls, but don't ever forget quality. Take your time where it counts, while maintaining your focus about making a sale.

SELECTIVITY

As you become established in your chosen business, you should become increasingly selective about your clientele. You will learn to spot and avoid potential problems. At first, your inclination will be to do business with almost anyone. But experience will teach you selectivity. What does this mean in practical terms? How do we know which people will be worthwhile clients?

Basically, you can select your own clients. An ideal customer is loyal, honest, pays bills on time, and doesn't cause major problems. If problems do arise, this type of client is understanding and patient. Unfortunately, there are not too many clients like this. I would rather have a $5,000 trouble-free customer than a $10,000 one who creates numerous problems for me and my company. The problems take up your time and energy, preventing you from developing additional business.

Consider the following examples: A potential customer is asking for things that you know will be difficult or impossible for your company to provide. Another potential customer continues to haggle over price long after you have made your final quote. A person tells you that if they have even a minor service problem, they will no longer do business with you. Someone else takes an unnecessary amount of your time to complain about minor problems. Another person tells you that they have problems with all of their vendors. In each of these cases, the customer can create more problems than their business is worth to you.

In advertising sales, for example, smaller advertisements might require far more attention than larger, more profitable ones. This is not to suggest that we only solicit high-volume customers. However, be attentive to the statements made by customers that might be indicative of potential problems. Through experience, we gradually learn to read the signs that a customer will be more trouble than they are worth. It is often greed that leads us to *indiscriminately* solicit new business. As our confidence and base business increase, we will be more willing to decline to do business with certain individuals. In doing so we free up energy for our better customers.

PART III

THE SALE

11

The
SALES
PRESENTATION

After you have gathered all of the pertinent information from the prospective customer, you then prepare a sales proposal. The sales presentation can be given at various times, depending on the type of business you're in. Here's how I do it in my business: I first conduct a premove survey. At that time, I ask the customer questions pertaining to their move. I survey both origin and destination conditions and compute an estimated cost of services. Next, I prepare and have typed a written proposal. Then I set up a meeting for a formal oral sales presentation.

The primary purpose of this presentation is to highlight the points of my proposal and to close the sale. Depending on how much preselling I have done in a particular case, the meeting can take several possible directions. However, the goal is to present my information with enthusiasm, professionalism, thoroughness, and clarity.

I usually begin with some type of icebreaker, rather than just launching into my presentation. Sometimes the customer will set the tone and pace through initial questions. If that happens, it is important to move at the customer's pace, not yours. As I go through the major points of my presentation, I watch the customer for visual cues such as confusion, delight, or discomfort. If I sense something, I will solicit questions or ask if they understand what I have been saying. Although I remain sensitive to the "agenda" of the client, I am quite assertive in making my presentations. I take charge and leave no doubt that it is my "show." I have been quite successful in beginning presentations with a very specific outline of what is unique about a particular client's situation, and how I am addressing their needs in my proposal. This is a key factor in my success. It is vitally important to focus in on the specific issues that are mentioned or highlighted by the customer. What makes them unique or is important to them? I try to get a feeling during the presentation, via their facial expressions and body language, about the customers' reactions.

Some common questions can give me a notion about their reactions to my presentation:

1. How does my proposal compare with others you have had thus far?

2. Do you have any reservations at all about using our company/product?

3. If you had to make a decision right now, how would we fare?

4. Do you have any questions at all that I haven't answered for you?

5. Would you feel comfortable using our company based on the information that you have?

The major tool in a sales presentation is what you say. However, you can enhance your words with videotape, flow charts, samples, and other audiovisual aids. They should be used to enhance, not replace, the oral presentation. The presentation should not be too technical nor too lengthy. It is wise to get a sense before you begin about how much time the customer has allotted for your sales presentation.

Before preparing for your presentation, you must determine the issues that are important to the decision maker. Some common issues are: price, guarantees, billing, and service. If the decision maker tells you that price isn't an issue, then don't focus on it. Thus, each sales presentation should be tailor-made for individual clients. You will lose many sales if the buyer senses that you are merely giving a memorized presentation that you use for everyone.

The way in which you present yourself reflects accordingly on the product/service that you represent. An oral presentation should be polished. It can provide showmanship and humor as well as the vital information about why the customer should select you. You should be fully prepared, and don't apologize for or demean your presentation. Put your best foot forward. And close the deal.

SHOWMANSHIP: THERE'S MORE BUSINESS WITH SHOW BUSINESS

A flair for the dramatic can enhance our overall sales presentation. In fact, anything we can do to stand apart from our competition in a positive way can increase our sales. Showmanship is one such way.

Showmanship can actually occur at any stage in the sales process. We can use it to get attention, either during a demonstration or during a formal sales presentation. It can be either planned or spontaneous. People love to be entertained. Ask yourself the question, "Who would you rather observe, a skilled entertainer or a person who is merely reciting product benefits in a boring monotone?" Not everyone has the skills to truly be a performer. But you can learn to add some dramatic touches to your selling presentation.

First of all, you have to find some aspect of your product/service that lends itself to a dramatic emphasis or presentation. Then you can experiment with techniques for presenting it. It could be a joke, an example, or any of a multitude of ways to draw attention to yourself and your product/service. The primary purpose of showmanship is to attract attention. Once you have accomplished that, you must then make a smooth transition back into the serious part of your business. If the customer seems to want more humor or dramatics, then give it to them. If not, then return to the presentation.

The main point here is that, with the proper use of showmanship, you can get the customer's attention and gain a step up on the competition. Use approaches that you feel comfortable with, and then assess how they work. Don't force a joke or a gimmick if the customer doesn't seem to want it. There is a time and place for everything. Experiment with new techniques periodically. And let the show go on.

REFERENCES AND REFERRALS

Positive references and referrals are critical to longevity and high levels of success. Without them, you must continually

generate all new business on your own. In order to get references and referrals, you must do a good job on the business you
get. The better the job you do, the better the references and the
more frequent the referrals. The time to solicit letters of
reference comes after you have proven yourself. Some satisfied
customers even write them without being asked. However, it is
to your benefit to take the initiative in gathering a substantial
file of letters from happy customers.

In addition to letters, you might list references with phone
numbers in your sales proposal. These people should be
informed that they might be receiving calls from prospective
customers. The list will be periodically updated and revised.
Take care to remove any names of customers who might have
taken their business elsewhere due to poor service. In
presenting references, it is quite important to be selective and
make them relevant to the new business that you're seeking.

Referrals can be the best possible source of new business.
Satisfied customers should be reminded about how much you
appreciate them. And when you do get referrals, it is very
important to personally thank the person giving the referral.
This show of appreciation is not only good manners, but can
generate future referrals. Some businesses pay referral fees, but
that's a matter of personal choice. However, you do need to
cultivate referral business in one way or another, and not just
assume that it will occur because you do a good job.

Customers need to be constantly reminded that you thrive
on their references and referrals. This gives them a feeling of
truly helping another person succeed and make money. In
many cases, referral business can virtually catapult a salesperson into a high level of success. So do a good job, remind the
customer if necessary that you are doing a good job, get the

references and referrals, and show your appreciation. If you learn how to do this effectively, your future is secure.

PROFILE 9—Maggie Gleeson
Using a Work Sample to Sell a Referred Client

Maggie Gleeson is not a salesperson, but continually uses sales skills to develop a client base in the field of psychotherapy. At a time when many therapists are seeing marked declines in their practices, hers is flourishing. How has she accomplished this? Well, she might get a client referred to her. She then calls them on the phone and demonstrates her concern and sensitivity in conversation. By focusing on the stated concerns of the person seeking therapy, she provides a work sample of what type of therapist she will be. She then discusses her fee schedule, and if they agree to commencing therapy, sets up the initial appointment. She has received no sales training, yet has learned, by way of a highly intuitive method, to increase her business. We don't often think of sales in this way, but this is one of many examples of how sales can be utilized in informal situations.

USING HUMOR IN SALES

One of my hobbies is comedy. In fact, I did stand-up comedy for a couple of years in nightclubs prior to entering sales. I believe that humor is one of the most powerful forms of interpersonal communication. Business people are often too serious. Some customers are really seeking some break in the routine of serious sales presentations. Lighten up a bit. I am not implying that you should not take your work seriously. You don't have to wear a flashing beanie during a sales presentation. Rather, you need to be able to determine when a bit of levity is appropriate. It could take the form of topical jokes, stories, or even impressions. Do what you feel comfortable with, no more, no less.

For myself, I am most comfortable with real life situations that are amusing to me. I am not really a joke teller. I do like to do impressions if I feel comfortable enough with the other person. Humor should not be forced, but should flow naturally from a situation. If you don't feel comfortable using humor, then don't do it.

Humor tends to relax people. However, in some cases, people find the inappropriate use of humor to be offensive. I cannot give you any hard and fast rules about using humor. My primary point here is that if you feel inclined to use it, there is a good chance that it can deepen rapport and set you apart from the deadly serious presentations of others.

12

CLOSING
THE SALE

Closing really begins with the initial contact with the prospective customer. In fact, everything you say and do after the initial contact contributes to the ultimate close. With this in mind, you must not wait until the last moment before trying to close a sale. Some of the more traditional approaches to sales consider the close a kind of do-or-die situation, where the customer is pressured to make a decision and sign the contract on the spot. My approach is much less pressured.

The customer needs to know that you want the business. Your job is to demonstrate your product and range of services in such a way as to leave no doubt that you should be the choice. You also prove yourself as a worthy candidate by returning calls promptly, keeping all commitments, and answering any questions or objections to the satisfaction of the customer. By the time you have arrived asking for the order, you have really done much of the closing already.

One useful technique is the trial close. You can use this at any juncture in the sales process. The trial close provides you with information about where you stand in the competition for the business. It can take several forms, including the following:

1. "If you had to make your decision today, how would we fare?"

2. "How do we stand?"

3. "Do you have any reasons why you wouldn't use our company?"

4. "Would you feel comfortable choosing my product?"

It is much better to get feedback via a trial close than to try to resurrect a sale after you have lost it or have been defeated by a competitor. Trial closing allows you to respond to any objections or alter your pricing before it's too late. Some customers give you clear signals about your chances of making a sale.

The more you know, the easier it is to make adjustments. The art of closing involves many factors. You cannot force a customer to buy from you. All you can do is present your information thoroughly, professionally, and enthusiastically. After you have done that, you can ask for the order. If you get a *yes*, you have successfully closed a sale. If you get a *no* or a *maybe*, then you need to know what you are lacking in order to get a favorable decision. In some cases you cannot do anything to change a *no* into a *yes*. But, in most cases, you can do at least something to make yourself more competitive.

One of the most difficult aspects of sales is determining exactly where you stand with a prospective customer. If you don't have this information, then you can't make the necessary adjustments to close a sale. Some customers refuse to share their decision-making criteria or objections. But with those who do, you can then attempt to convince them they should buy from you.

There is a point during the close where you must have faith that you have given a superior sales effort and back off. If you've done your job to the best of your ability, then additional effort can be counterproductive. You should not push people too hard; they will tend to consider this as a negative factor. The ideas I'm expressing here represent the core philosophy of this book. You should consider "pulling" the customer to your point of view rather than "pushing" them.

When you're in the process of closing a sale, it's important to relax and to appear confident. At this point, the customer needs to feel good about choosing you. Don't get overanxious to sign the contract. Do everything in your power to solidify the customer's decision by providing an attitude of confidence and security. Then make sure that you deliver on your promises.

OVERCOMING OBJECTIONS

One of the major attributes of a superior salesperson is the ability to consistently overcome buyer objections. This skill is one of the most difficult to develop. It takes a high level of product knowledge, patience, and persistence. In many cases, closing a sale is simply a matter of satisfactorily answering objections. In order to overcome objections, we must first determine what they are.

Some of the most common buyer objections are as follows:

1. The price is too high.

2. The quality of all products/services being compared is equal.

3. The customer is happy with a competitor currently being used.

4. Not enough benefits have been demonstrated.

5. The customer doesn't need our product/service.

The message in all of these cases is essentially the same. The prospective customer is really saying, "Sell me." And that is precisely your job at that point in time. The burden of proof is squarely upon the shoulders of the salesperson. Your job is to convince the customer beyond a shadow of a doubt that their objection is unfounded or tenuous. Herein lies one of the most difficult aspects of the entire selling process.

The price objection is perhaps the most common. How often do you hear the statement, "Your price is too high?" When you do, there are several things that you must do. First of all, you should determine whether or not they have done any comparison shopping. If they haven't, then you can begin by informing them about industry standards for rates. If they have, then you primarily need to prove why your price is fair. In addition, you must convincingly demonstrate exactly what you are offering for your price. You need to sell service rather than the lowest price. Buyers often need to be educated about quality of service and how the lowest prices are not deals at all in many cases.

Sometimes the price objection is simply a matter of mathematics. That is, you must explain to the buyer exactly how the figures were derived and how they might be varied or reduced. The last thing you want to do is give up or retreat when you hear the price objection. It has aptly been stated that the sales process truly begins with the initial rejection.

The second common objection is that all competitors are equal. That is, in the customer's mind, a coin could be tossed to make the decision. In this case, your primary job is to demonstrate the salient benefits of your product/service. You must do so with conviction, clarity, and enthusiasm. In your presentation, you need to continually emphasize the various ways in which your product/service is clearly superior to that of your competitors. As you go through your reasons, try to get some agreement from the customer. Don't make it a monologue.

The third objection is one of the most difficult to overcome. When the customer is using another product/ service and is happy with it, you have your work cut out for you. In some cases this objection is too powerful to overcome immediately. But you can begin by attempting to find at least some aspect of their current vendor with which they are dissatisfied. If you can find something, then you can work on that and try to demonstrate your superiority in that area.

Another approach is not to try to persuade them too strongly at the moment, but to work at being a backup in case of any service breakdowns with their current product/service. This latter approach shows a respect for their loyalty and to the competitor, and can actually be better in the long run. If a prospective customer tells me that they have been using a competitor for a period of time and that they are quite happy with their current level of service and price, I would rather be a backup than be rejected outright for being too pushy.

In the fourth type of objection, we might not get the message as directly as: "You have not shown me enough benefits." But if you sense that your prospect wants to buy from you but won't sign the contract yet, then you probably *haven't* demonstrated enough benefits. Try to pinpoint which types of benefits seem to appeal to the prospect. Then focus in on those areas until you feel that you have hit a "hot button."

The final type of objection we will consider is when the customer claims that he or she doesn't need our product/ service. This does not necessarily apply to all fields—for example my own. People must move and are therefore only making a decision about which professional mover to select. The only time it might apply is when they are considering a self-move. In that case, I might point out to them in a helpful way, the potential difficulties in the actual execution of a move. In many sales areas, you are trying to convince the prospect that they need your product/service and that yours is the best that money can buy. The *need* area is a difficult one. Basically, you should demonstrate how your product/service can improve the potential customer's quality of life. Offering a trial period is an excellent technique for establishing a need.

Ten years ago, I didn't think I needed either a videocassette recorder or a word processor. After having acquired both, I developed an appreciation for them that I would never have had without the experience of using them. So, allowing the prospect to use something prior to buying it can assist immeasurably in establishing a need. In cases where you are unable to do this, then you might suggest they observe your company *in action*, if possible, to assess your level of excellence. I will often invite prospects to observe a relocation prior to making their decision.

The ability to effectively overcome objections is an essential skill in improving sales performance. You will never advance beyond mediocrity if you don't learn how to anticipate and answer objections. This is one of the most difficult aspects of the entire sales process. Master it, and you will be enormously successful. It is often important to anticipate certain objections so that we have rehearsed at least the general nature of our response. This is a better response than to be caught by surprise with an objection that you hadn't anticipated at all.

Exercise 9—Overcoming Common Objections

As discussed above, one of the most difficult aspects of selling is to effectively overcome buyer objections to our product/service. Truly successful sales professionals know what common objections they're likely to encounter. And they're ready with practiced responses to those objections. What objections do you get regarding your product/service? In this exercise, develop a persuasive response to each of the following objections. Then ask yourself if your prospective customers would be satisfied with your responses. This is a wonderful and fun activity to role play with other people. One person (the prospect) states the objection, and the other person (the salesperson) responds.

Objection 1 *—Your price is too high.*

Objection 2 *— I'm already doing business with someone else and am quite satisfied with their service.*

Objection 3 *—You're all really close. I think I'll just flip a coin to make my decision.*

Objection 4 *—I've had some problems with your service in the past.*

Objection 5 *—Your billing and payment period are too short for us.*

Objection 6 *—I need some time to think about this.*

Objection 7 *—I just don't feel right about your product.*

Objection 8 *—Your competitor has a better warranty program.*

Objection 9 *—I really don't need your product/service.*

Objection 10 *—Why should I buy from you?*

PROFILE 10—Craig Fulmer
The Closer

Craig Fulmer is an individual who I trained in office moving sales. Prior to joining our company, he sold food products to restaurants. He is thirty-nine years old, the father of three sons, and a top notch golfer. When he entered the moving business, he had virtually no product knowledge. However, he did have prior sales experience. He knew what it took to close sales.

What is it that he has or does to write business? Primarily, it's the ability to zero in on the concerns of the potential customers and to respond to those concerns. He takes enough time and care preparing rate quotations and has excellent attention to detail. Another technique that assists Craig in closing sales is that he follows up with potential customers after the initial meeting and presentation of the proposal. He uses the phone and mail to communicate effectively.

In addition to these factors, his determination to close the sale is crucial to his high closing ratio. He is available to the customer prior to the decision, and always returns calls promptly. When objections are raised, he is well equipped to answer them. Above all, he is not shy about asking for the order. In sum, he provides the customer with the assurance that he will handle their business with care.

TYPES OF BUYERS AND DECISION MAKING STRATEGIES

In order to be effective in sales, you need to understand some of the basic types of buyers you are likely to encounter. I'm speaking here in general types rather than specific cases. After a while you'll learn to identify some of these types and to vary your sales approach accordingly.

Type 1—The Impulsive Buyer

This type of buyer makes buying decisions on impulse. This can work in your favor, except that decisions are sometimes reversed on impulse as well. In general, the impulse buyer operates much more on emotion than reason. There might be some pondering that goes on, but the actual decisions are made on impulse. Often, the impulse buyer doesn't care to hear your presentation. They are anxious to buy, and it is your job to keep up with their pace, but without rushing yourself. They might even tell you that they are not doing any other shopping. The business is yours for the asking. However, if you get too hurried or greedy, you can lose the order just as quickly as you got it.

Type 2—*The Haggler*

The haggler will work you for your lowest price and best deal. They will often go back and forth between you and your competitor until they have squeezed every penny out of you. Their decision is almost always based on price. But in addition to price, they are often just looking for someone who's willing to haggle back with them. If you are too easy in reducing your price it could jeopardize the sale. This type of customer can be dangerous, and loyalty is based solely on the bottom line. Even if you give superb service and quality, you'll be just another memory if you can't compete on the issue of price.

Type 3—*The Cogitator*

The cogitator takes much time to make a decision, going through a long period of clarification with the various competitors. This type of buyer is the opposite of the impulse buyer. Once you have secured their business, they are typically very loyal. However, beware of the ones who not only take forever to make their initial decision but who make you go through the whole process again on each subsequent occasion. It's important not to rush this type of buyer, lest they eliminate you from contention. They tend to be very logical, and therefore susceptible to logical sales techniques.

Type 4—*The Naive Buyer*

The naive buyer knows little or nothing about your product/service. Your primary job here is to be an educator. You need to inform the buyer honestly about your product/service. You must also suggest criteria for making the decision which will work in your favor. Usually, the salesperson who does the best job of teaching secures the order.

Type 5—*The Manipulator*

This type of buyer uses the power of their position to make you "jump through hoops" and do a series of tasks of marginal importance to prove how much you want the order. Often they make you revise your proposal to make sure that you're willing to play their game. I have very little patience with this type of buyer. However, if the order is large enough, I sometimes play the game, but try to keep the manipulation to a minimum.

Type 6—The Buying Team

This is a situation where you have more than one person who is making the buying decision. There are infinite variations on this theme. However, your primary concern in these cases is to consider every decision maker, especially those with higher status. At some point, you must take a stand, and hope that you make the correct statements. This situation is especially difficult when the various buyers have clearly different buying motives. It's also useful to try to determine some of the possible group dynamics and how the various players might influence each other in arriving at a final decision.

Type 7—*The Communicator*

The communicator is a buyer who tells you up front exactly what the criteria are for making the decision. Your job is to listen carefully and to develop a sales proposal and presentation that meets those criteria. This is one of the easiest situations to sell in, except that your competition has the same advantages as you do.

Type 8—*The Fogger*

The fogger is the exact opposite of the communicator. He or she doesn't tell you anything about decision-making criteria. In these cases, you need to ask many questions and try to read between the lines to determine what the criteria are.

Type 9—*The Liar Buyer*

The liar buyer tells you one thing about the criteria for the decision, then makes the decision based on something entirely different. Forget them. They are not worth your effort and will cause you problems somewhere down the line. You don't need their business.

Type 10—*The Reactionary Buyer*

This type of buyer makes decisions on the basis of problems they have had with previous vendors. If they had a problem with late deliveries, then they might choose a new vendor who proves that they will *never* be late. The problem with this type of buyer is that they often make unrealistic assumptions about their new vendor. Be careful not to enter any agreements under false pretenses.

We have considered ten major types of buyers. There are other types that you may have encountered. Keep your eyes and ears open for the wide variety of characteristics and decision-making strategies out there. This will guide you in your future sales efforts.

13

SERVICING YOUR ACCOUNTS

Essential to Longevity

PROFILE 11—Andrea Evensen
Inducing Loyalty in the Prospective Buyer by
Being a Helper

In the process of buying a house, my wife and I were introduced to a real estate broker through a referral from a friend. Other than our friend's recommendation, we had no reason to have any strong pressure to use Andrea or to have any loyalty toward her. However, she did several impressive things. First of all, upon learning what my occupation was, she immediately put me in touch with someone in my field who could award me business. Second, she provided us with a tremendous amount of information that was invaluable in isolating neighborhoods with homes that fit our requirements. She came across as a helper first and a salesperson second. This quality was quite endearing, and she was sincere about it. She made it clear that the kind of relationship that she wanted to build with us was for the long haul, not just for a quick sale.

SALES IS SERVICE

Sales is service! Now that you've closed a sale, you may think that your job is done. But it's at this point that the *real* process of selling begins. It is your job to make certain that your customers receive what you promise them. Effective servicing of accounts separates the average from the exceptional salespeople. Servicing your accounts does much to develop rapport and to cement a long-term business relationship. In my business, it involves several things:

1. Being present during major moves and making an appearance during smaller ones.

2. Keeping my client abreast of rate changes, discounting, and billing procedures.

3. Providing a thorough and timely planning and organizational set-up for each move in order to prepare the move coordinator in regards to relevant details of move procedures.

4. Responding quickly to the client's questions, requests, and problems.

5. Taking the client to lunch periodically.

6. Giving the client complimentary tickets to sporting events, productions, or special events that they've expressed an interest in.

7. Giving the client a variety of promotional gifts such as calendars, coasters, miniature trucks, and pens.

8. Calling periodically, whether the client is giving us business or not.

9. Sending birthday and holiday cards and gifts.

10. Bringing pastries or a favorite food to the client.

All of these things have the effect of making the client feel good and comfortable doing business with you. They keep your name in front of the client in a variety of ways. You need to think creatively about ways in which you can service your accounts that might be different from mine. Some examples are: mailers; newsletters; and account outings, like boat cruises, train rides, and parties. The critical fact here is that your job only begins when you are awarded an account. It is the level of service you provide after you get the business that determines your ultimate level of success.

Providing high quality service has a positive side effect for you. By immersing yourself in the product/ service, you increase your product knowledge, while providing service at the same time. You will build your base of business by continuing to provide good service and getting your satisfied customers to give you references and referrals.

A true professional knows how much time and involvement are required to guarantee good service. It involves much more than merely showing up for public relations. You need to become deeply involved in the operational end of your own company to ensure that quality service is being rendered. Service your inside support personnel (secretaries, dispatcher, receptionist) also. And in a service field, it is vital to have a very positive working relationship with your crews and supervisors. Buy them donuts, lunch, drinks, and anything else that lets them know they are appreciated by you. Service is absolutely critical to sales success. Many average salespeople can secure accounts. However, it takes an exceptional salesperson to maintain accounts over a long period of time.

FOLLOW THROUGH AND THROUGH AND THROUGH: YOU'RE *NEVER* THROUGH

An important characteristic of successful salespeople is continual follow-through. When average salespeople stop, thinking they're finished with a job, high achievers continue to follow through. Beginners mistakenly think that calling on an account two or three times will get them the business. In some rare cases this is true. However, to acquire and maintain significant and profitable repeat business accounts, regular and long-term follow-through is necessary.

Follow-through refers to repeated, sequential steps taken over a period of time to secure and maintain business. Some common forms are:

1. Follow-up letters to meetings

2. Phone calls to solicit questions regarding buyer objections

3. Periodic in-person calls

4. Regularly scheduled phone calls

5. Checking orders before and after they are delivered

All of these and other techniques are designed to maintain contact and rapport with customers. Once again, quality of service is demonstrated in follow-through. Rather than merely going after numerous new accounts, it is critical to follow through deeply and consistently with existing ones.

In developing an overall sales strategy, you should plan your follow-up activities ahead of time and keep them varied. It is so easy to lose touch if a concrete schedule is not made and kept. My own personal style and technique allow for continual revision and variation in that schedule as I go along. For example, when I am very busy with current business, I will postpone a second or less urgent call. I periodically group my calls by such categories as:

1. cold call

2. lead sources

3. call for appointments for surveys

4. urgent calls

5. by profession

6. by territory

7. repeat business accounts

8. will-calls (people who are supposed to call me back)

Follow-through involves a deepening of a relationship. It is more than merely "checking in" with the customer. The goal is to progress toward a sale. Follow-through also involves honoring your commitments. People who keep their promises in a timely manner secure and maintain business. Take the extra step. Stay in touch. When you think you are finished, take another step. Use your imagination. Set aside some free time to let your individual creativity work. Try new ideas occasionally; take some risks. Make yourself and your product/service stand out from your competitors. As long as you're in sales, you're never through. Prices change, decision makers change, and situations change. Use these opportunities to be an agent of change yourself. If you do all of this, you will get the business. And then your work begins.

BEING THERE: MAKING IT EASY TO BUY FROM YOU

When I walk into most stores, I need a certain amount of assistance. It bothers me when I have to conduct a "search and destroy" mission just to find an available salesperson. For my own tastes, the ideal person is immediately available but not pushy. I give my business to people who make it easy for me to buy. Effective salespeople are indeed "helpers," in much the same way that therapists and nurses are. They are there when you need them to assist you in solving your problems. Many mediocre salespeople do not reach excellence because they don't understand this basic fact. Closing is really opening; it marks the true beginning of a business relationship.

In my business, it is vital to be readily available to prospective customers, especially when they are at the stage of making a decision. I must be responsive to the needs of a customer. Some customers are demanding and even unreasonable. They might put you off for months or even years. Then, all of a sudden, they want you at their immediate service on very short notice. You may not particularly like this, but you'll respond if you want the business. There have been numerous occasions when my consistent callbacks have yielded sales for me over competitors who quit calling or responded too slowly or insufficiently.

Some customers are simply lazy, and feel they shouldn't have to make any effort to buy something. Because of this, you must continue to call on them until they are willing to meet with you. Persistence pays many dividends, especially when coupled with patience and confidence. You should develop a system that records and monitors your callbacks. Continuing to put new prospects into your system will always pay rewards.

It is helpful to ask potential customers how often you should call back when soliciting business. You must be sensitive to their needs and concerns other than those relating to your product. It will help you if you have some empathy for the customer's needs and problems.

Timing is very important in prospecting and soliciting. You need to be there when your customer needs you. Keep careful records and respond within the promised time commitment. Call or arrive when you say you will do so. If you make your customer comfortable and instill confidence, you will be extremely successful in sales.

CONSISTENCY: SUSTAINED EFFORTS YIELD RESULTS

Top sales producers have several traits in common. One of them is consistency of effort. This refers to a regular, sustained work ethic over a prolonged period of time. Because sales results do not occur overnight, it is necessary to have work habits that are consistent. What does this mean in practice?

Commission sales allows for a substantial amount of schedule flexibility and personal freedom. If abused, however, this freedom will lead to low sales production. There are peak selling hours in all fields. In food service, meal times are obviously vital; a dinner house must be geared up for the dinner hours. In selling to most businesses, the hours between 8:30 and 11:30 a.m, and 1:30 and 4:30 p.m. are considered peak. Before or after those times you might not be able to find the buyer. Therefore, calculations, sales reports, proposals, and transcriptions of notes should be done during non-peak hours or meal times.

There will be times at which our energy levels, for various reasons, fluctuate. We will probably be highly motivated after a big sale. However, it is important to work at a fairly consistent pace, day after day, week after week, month after month. Most jobs have clearly scheduled hours. Because most sales jobs don't, naive salespeople interpret this as a license to be lazy. Effort should be fairly consistent. Not too rigid, but regular. You can't do everything in one or two days. You must remain available to set appointments at your customer's convenience, not yours.

Phone calling provides a good example for the importance of consistency of effort. If you attempt to do all of your calling on one day, you might seem too rushed. If you have thirty calls to make, two days might allow a more reasonable period of time than one day to accomplish this task. It brings back the issue of quality versus quantity discussed in Chapter 10. Our moods change also, and perhaps the second day will bring a better frame of mind. Rome wasn't built in a day. Neither is a successful sales career. It takes time.

One of the most difficult aspects of sales jobs is managing and structuring time. When you develop a consistent work schedule, you will have more time per day to accomplish your goals. Plan to work every day (except possibly on weekends), at least in the beginning stages of your career. Once you have established yourself on solid ground, then you can take some time off. Remain open to schedule changes, unforeseen events, and meetings which are longer or shorter than anticipated. You can save some of your tasks to fill in time between appointments. Accomplish something positive every day that you work. Success is a direct by-product of a consistent sales effort.

Consistency does not mean that some days aren't longer or more critical than others. Rather, it means that you don't try to force all of your appointments into one day for your own convenience. Take the examples of dieting and staying in physical condition. Most successful programs are long-term, emphasizing the development of habits that lead to weight loss and maintenance. Starving yourself or lifting massive amounts of weights one day a week is dangerous. In sales, it is best to stay fairly even-tempered through successes and failures. Continue to work after a major sale. It is fine to celebrate, but one sale won't last forever. Work consistently and success will be yours.

PART IV

PUTTING IT ALL TOGETHER

14

LONGEVITY
It Pays to Stay Put
for a While

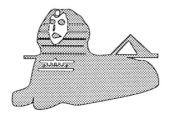

One way to become successful in sales is merely to stay with one company for a period of years. This may sound simplistic, but it's true. For those of you who are new to sales, I advise you to select your company carefully. Don't believe for an instant that you can "get to the top" by job-hopping. Some change may be desirable, but for the most part you should make about a ten year commitment to a company. What does this do for you?

First of all, you can build up a solid clientele that is based upon strong personal and business relationships. It takes approximately three years in most businesses to develop a cadre of accounts and referrals. Any time you make a company change, you are susceptible to losing some of your accounts. In some sad cases, you lose all of them. Of course, if you have developed solid accounts, you should be able to take some or all of them with you to your new company. You must have a strong rapport with your accounts. If you don't, then the business remains tenuous.

Often you'll do business with a customer who then keeps your business card. It might be five years before they call you again. If you have made a switch in companies, it's likely that they'll have a hard time reaching you at your new company. Many sales-oriented businesses simply refuse to provide customers with the new phone numbers of departed sales-people. It's up to you to keep in contact, either through the mail, phone, or in person. Staying with one company tends to establish you as a person of stability and integrity. People know where to find you. In addition, you'll even get some business based on longevity alone.

In my own case, I began to see consistent repeat business in my third year, and a substantial increase in the fifth year. People could find Bill Saleebey, and most of that repeat or referral business was less problematic than new business. In my early years, it was more difficult to secure new business due to inexperience and lack of product knowledge. But, each time I serviced some of the "old" business, it solidified the bond and broadened my business base. Are you getting the picture? You're far better off seeing sales as a career than as a temporary way to make money.

By committing yourself to a company, you also increase your own belief in that organization, as well as your subsequent ability to sell. This philosophy tends to make you more patient. By understanding that true success takes time, you will then be less frantic to make a particular sale. This entire concept of longevity focuses your attention on the long-term returns from your ever-increasing effort, skill, and overall sales results.

Instead of thinking in terms of weeks and months, you will think in terms of years and five-year periods. When I finally decided to change companies, I mistakenly did so in somewhat of a hurry. Consequently, I was unable to warn my long-term customers. I did eventually contact most of them and advise them of my change. However, in some cases, my planning was insufficient to keep the account with me at my new company. Additionally, there were some contacts that I didn't keep track of when changing companies, and I lost some of those potential calls also. So, it's very important to plan ahead for a change as much as possible.

PATIENCE

My father used to say to me, "Patience is rewarding." No statement is truer for the sales professional, who must be able to wait for experience, knowledge, time and success to reach fruition in the form of a high sales volume. It is vital for salespeople to develop an inner confidence in their ultimate success. If they lack patience, salespeople are doomed to failure and the inevitable return to guaranteed-salary positions.

What does it really mean to be patient? First of all, the beginning salesperson must have either some financial cushion (i.e., savings) or a guaranteed salary or sales draw in order to feel relaxed enough to function effectively. You need to fully understand the differences between a straight commission position, base pay plus commission, draws with paybacks, and advances against future commissions. Every company defines these options a bit differently. Know what type of compensation program you're getting into before you sign any contracts. It's wise to get a guarantee that will cover your monthly bills with a slight cushion. Some pressure is motivating, but excessive pressure can lead to counter-productive behavior, psychosomatic illnesses, or disruptive stress. This doesn't mean that the salesperson need not have any urgency to sell. But there is usually a certain period of time before commissions provide enough money to meet financial obligations on a consistent basis. Some sacrifice may be necessary before an acceptable income level is reached. Hence, the need for patience.

Lack of patience causes most beginning salespeople to quit before they achieve consistent success. True patience is born of an inner faith and confidence in one's ability to succeed. Steady increases in sales are noticed and charted. Closing ratios are plotted. It helps immensely to have a sales manager encourage you if you lose your confidence or vision. Ultimate success can be reached by continual effort and self-improvement. I was strongly motivated by observing the successes of fellow salespeople in my company. I figured if they could succeed, then so could I.

It takes a lot of strength and courage to continue to sell in the face of minimal returns. Being patient does not mean to continue when there is strong evidence that you're not making any improvement. However, you need to set some limits for yourself. That's often a difficult to do without being able to predict the future. Ask others, such as your sales manager and other successful salespeople in your company, how long you might have to wait before you are earning an acceptable level of income.

Patience also applies to individual accounts. Sometimes it takes years before you secure an account. With patience and consistent effort, you will win many accounts including the larger, more difficult ones to secure. If you're willing to wait, and willing to work hard and consistently, then you'll receive the rewards you so richly deserve.

LEARNING FROM EXPERIENCE

How do we improve our sales performance? One of the major ways to better yourself is to learn from both positive and negative experiences. To do this, you must be continually attuned to the various reasons for your sales successes and failures. You need to find out why you close sales as well as why you lose them. When you close a sale, the customer can be asked at an opportune time why you were selected. But even when they give their answer, you should know that there might be other reasons they are not conscious of or that they are unwilling to share with you.

When I make a sale, I make it a point to ask the customer why I was chosen. Sometimes the reasons surprise me. But I am then able to add them to the potential strengths that I carry into a sales opportunity. The most common reasons I have been given are the following:

1. The customer felt comfortable with me.

2. I projected confidence and professionalism.

3. I took time with the customer and answered all questions thoroughly.

4. I always arrived on time and kept my commitments.

5. My sales presentation was clear, informative, and thorough.

6. The customer liked me.

7. My proposal was complete and addressed the issues that were important to the customer.

8. My references were relevant and very positive.

9. I mentioned benefits that were omitted by my competitors.

10. The customer believed and trusted in me.

11. I was genuinely enthusiastic about my service.

12. I developed a proposal that addressed the specific needs of the client.

13. I followed up consistently.

14. I responded in a timely manner.

15. I demonstrated more knowledge of specific issues than my competitors.

Learning from negative experiences is often more difficult than learning from successes. For one thing, the customer who has decided not to buy from you is sometimes reluctant to tell the reasons. But you can deduce them if you are able to find out why your competitor was selected. Rarely will the customer tell you that you were just outsold. Usually I get information about the following:

1. The customer got a better deal.

2. The competitor had a better proposal, presentation, or offered a specific thing that I didn't.

3. The boss chose another company because of a personal contact.

4. The decision was made by someone other than my contact.

5. The company is not going to use any professional movers.

As time goes on, you will become increasingly familiar with the reasons for your successes and failures. You need to work to improve on weak areas, or you will continue to lose sales for the same reasons. You also need to know clearly why you *are* making sales so that you continue to develop your strengths. Ask customers about your performance. It's the best way to learn from your experience, and to improve yourself.

15

HOW TO GET OUT of A SELLING SLUMP

If you are just starting in sales, you might not have experienced a selling slump. But if you have, you know how discouraging it can be. Nothing seems to go right. You feel a bit like Rodney Dangerfield, getting "no respect." What does an athlete do to get out of a slump? Several things are known to help. The first is to determine what, if anything in particular, they are doing wrong. Then they practice continually until they get out of the slump. But besides the possible mechanical or technical problems, mental problems can make the slump continue. They get overly anxious, press too hard, and the slump persists.

In sales, the situation is somewhat similar. But the first step is to figure out what you are doing right, what attitudes and methods got you the business when you *were* closing sales. Don't change everything because you're in a slow period. Determine what you might be doing wrong, and work to change it. And, like the athlete, practice, practice, practice. In addition, try not to get too down on yourself. It could be things external to yourself that might be causing the slump. The economy might be down, it could be off-season for your product/service, or you might be suffering a delayed reaction to a vacation that you took months ago, when you didn't make any calls at all for two weeks. You need to be an effective troubleshooter to determine the exact nature of your problem so that you can correct it.

Above all, you must continue to work harder than ever before. There is no substitute for hard, consistent work. Work is practice. When you stop working, you tend to think too much about things that might not be related to your problem at all. It also helps to talk with fellow salespeople and your sales manager to get some ideas that you might not have considered. We often misdiagnose our problems and change aspects of our approach that should not be changed at all.

Another thing you can do during a slump is reactivate the components of selling that you might not be practicing, such as: prospecting, administering, entertaining, and re-calling on pending accounts. When I'm in a slump or slow period, my best remedy is to go back to cold calling. If that doesn't work, then I go through my business cards or lead sources and reestablish contact. I invariably find something that gets me back on track. But in all cases I do something to accelerate the process. Once I start selling again, I work very hard to keep up the momentum and try to guard against future slumps by increased effort and awareness. You must be creative and open to even the most unlikely cause of your slump. Experiment with that "crazy idea" that you've had for months. It might just be what breaks you out of your slow period. Don't give up or mope. Those are self-defeating behaviors that only prolong the slump. Get off your chair and sell.

OVERCOMING BOREDOM: VARY YOUR APPROACH

Like many salespeople, I'm easily bored. When I've conducted several surveys in a morning, I tend to lose interest and get lost in the mechanical process. There is a certain amount of routine and repetition in any job (though typically less in sales careers). You must accept some routine. However, you can do certain things to reduce the potential for boredom. First and foremost, you can vary your approach and routine. Don't do the same thing every day. If you are not required to go into the office every day, don't. You can cold call one day, administer the next, and sell the next. Go into new areas periodically. Whenever you find yourself getting bored, do something to vary your routine. It will usually get you out of the rut.

Sometimes just imagining past sales successes can begin to trigger the positive juices that can quell a slump. We tend to lose sight of better times and get mired in the haze of the slump. Remember those better times, and try to think of anything you might have done to create those feelings. Use your imagination to burst you out of the bubble of inertia.

16

SALES REPORTS AND RECORD KEEPING

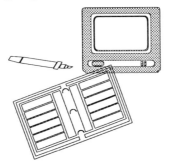

M any salespeople get bogged down or irritated with paperwork, especially with the sales reports required by their sales managers. Part of the reason for these reactions is that the sales reports can present an honest picture of what and how you are really doing. We may not want to look at our actual level of production, particularly at the earlier stages in our careers. Another reason is that we are not organized, and sales reports seem like just another bit of busywork in an already busy schedule.

Personally, I find that sales reports can provide valuable information about improvement in closing ratios and about demographics, as well as other data that can be utilized in modifying our sales plan. Granted, the reports take time. But they do show us where we are in our development. My method is to try to keep up with my reports on a daily basis so that the task doesn't become overwhelming. When I set up an appointment, I enter it into my sales report immediately. Then, when I get the results, I fill it in. Basically, the sales reports are for you. Although they might be required by your sales manager or department, you should see them as a learning tool for yourself.

Record keeping can assist you greatly in getting yourself organized. By maintaining records and files, you are then able to find data when you need it. Whether you use paper or a computer, you need to keep track of what you're doing. However, you must not let record keeping activities detract from selling time. Evenings and weekends can be ideal for catching up without the pressure of time you might face during prime selling time. Once again, you will benefit from a system of record keeping. Although you may have begun keeping records because it was required by others, you can chart your direction and progress by referring to these records. If you aren't satisfied with the forms your company uses, you can develop your own which allow for more meaningful information about your selling habits.

Don't fight your sales manager in terms of reports that are required of you. Rebellion is self-defeating. Always keep in mind that you should be working for yourself, and that your sales manager is someone to assist you in reaching your potential. As you improve, the reports will be easier to complete. And, as I pointed out above, by referring to your records you can determine what areas need improvement. You can learn about your progress, and increase your sales.

It is helpful to periodically review past sales reports to look specifically for trends in terms of geographic strengths and weaknesses, actual closing ratio, average number of appointments per month, reasons for closing or not closing sales, and any other pertinent information that *you* can use to improve your performance.

You can set up data bases on your computer to keep track of a variety of sales-related information. The emphasis should be on *useful* information. The time spent on inputting and referring to this data should never cut into prime selling time. You can do some of this on a trial-and-error basis, continually analyzing the usefulness of the information for assessing sales trends and *improving sales performance.*

17

The SALES ASSISTANT/SECRETARY Taking Care of Your Business While YOU are SELLING

I have been extremely fortunate to have a highly effective sales assistant/secretary/inside support person. (I will be utilizing the female pronouns not to reflect any gender bias, but because my assistants have been women.) Much of what she does is vitally helpful to my overall sales effort. What does she do? First of all, she completes sales proposals and rate quotations promptly. She's courteous and patient with customers, while always maintaining a loyalty to me. Overall, her efforts allow me to generate and sell new business.

Her attitude is consistently positive. She performs tasks without complaining in the slightest. In addition, she takes initiative to perform critical activities without being asked to do so. I don't have to spend undue time explaining details to her. She can "read between the lines" and complete projects without being monitored. A major reason for her effectiveness is that she possesses an in-depth understanding of the business. This knowledge allows her to make intelligent decisions in my absence.

What can a salesperson do to develop an able assistant? Part of the answer lies in hiring someone who is intelligent, cooperative, courteous, sales-oriented, and motivated. With good "raw material," you can then train the person in your way of conducting business. It's important not to be unreasonable in your requests. There are several major things that can be done to properly teach an assistant, such as:

1. Tell them what you expect of them.

2. Reward good effort and performance.

3. Correct mistakes gently and unemotionally if possible.

4. Demonstrate what you want done as clearly as you can.

5. Spend some time in informal conversation. Take a genuine interest in their life.

A sales assistant, if properly trained and nurtured, can be extremely valuable to a salesperson. Your business is entrusted to them on a daily basis. A good sales assistant can not only maintain your current business but also be instrumental in securing new business. They need to be informed about important incoming phone calls, correspondences, and other matters. Communication is the key to this matter. You should take your assistant to lunch periodically, and try to remember birthdays, anniversaries, and other important events. Being thoughtful will help in developing a strong bond between the two of you.

18

TRAINING OTHERS

You might be wondering about this chapter being in a how-to-sell book. But the concept is actually quite powerful. As you master the various aspects of selling, sharing this information with others has a strong reinforcing effect. I had my first opportunity to train someone only two years into my own sales career. At that point I still had much to learn myself. But even then I was able to communicate the knowledge I did possess.

Training others forces you to become aware all of the various bits of knowledge and techniques of the sales process. Your training doesn't have to be fully completed for you to assist in the training of others. What is important is that you share what you do know, as well as the aspects of sales that might still be somewhat confusing to you. You need to differentiate between these two areas for the trainee. By sharing your understanding and experiences, you strengthen your foundations. You also have the opportunity to learn about the developmental process of the trainee. You can do problem solving and brainstorming with the trainee about different ways to secure sales.

My strength in training is in the sharing of information and experiences. I enjoy helping others to gain the benefits of sales. My major weakness is in the detail work. This also happens to be my major weakness in selling. Another weakness is monitoring the behavior of another. I realize that some of this is desirable or necessary, but my approach is more permissive.

Another major aspect of my training style is to give support and positive feedback to the trainee. I feel that this is incredibly vital to the learning process. It's important to be positive, specially at the beginning stages of training. Criticism can come gradually, but not too much in the beginning.

One of the key elements of sales training is direct communication. I find this is best achieved at breakfast or lunch meetings. There is something of a bonding effect when you "break bread" with someone. It gets you out of the office, and you have the opportunity to share something of your personal as well as professional life. We are people before we are salespeople. This fact should never be forgotten. A trainer should be sensitive to the personal lives of trainees.

Sharing is the essence of training. There are few secrets. If you have ideas that can help another salesperson, it is to the benefit of both of you to share them. By doing this, you not only help the trainee, but you also help yourself. We never stop learning. I continue to interact and share information with former trainees. I still learn from them as well. Training is a two-way street. You both give and receive when you are involved in learning.

Effective sales training involves attention to both the sales process and the specific sales situations that confront trainees. It's fine to discuss the theories of selling, but theory without practice is not very helpful. Much benefit can be derived from the analysis of specific cases and situations that are actually confronting either the trainer or trainee. Above all, sales training involves the clear sharing of pertinent information of how sales are made, coupled with specific techniques that lead to those sales.

CONCLUSION

So you thought sales was easy. Well it is, really, if you understand why people buy and what you should think, say, and do as a salesperson. You should never forget that your ultimate sales approach will be unique to you. It is something that you will develop over a period of years. Others will guide, cajole, and even mislead you. But you must stay on the path that is most likely to lead to your success. It's important to be true to yourself and to your own gut feelings. You'll increase your confidence in your own judgment with time and experience. It's helpful to get the feedback of others, but it's equally important to develop your own ability to assess situations that are likely to arise.

Your eventual level of productivity is primarily based on your effort and ability. There may be some valid excuses for low sales levels, but not many. You can determine your own destiny and earnings. You have the power to exert a strong control over your career in sales. I sincerely hope that you can attain some of the many benefits that are available to you. Your sales career will allow you flexibility of schedule, contact with a wide array of people, and the opportunity to make a lot of money. Sales is challenging and fun. Use these ideas, reread this book, and sell. Your growth and development as a salesperson will provide you with a rewarding career. Be patient and you will reap many rewards, both financial and personal.

If you have a quality product/service, present yourself in a professional manner, and practice the techniques in this book, you will be successful. You will not sell to everyone you attempt to sell to. But if you treat people in a humanistic way, listen to them carefully, and respond to their needs, your sales will steadily increase. Be realistic and patient. The best situation is to experience a steady increase that does not overwhelm you or your company. You want to be able to effectively service the business that you do write. Get to know yourself and your customers, and use this knowledge to improve your performance. I wish you tremendous success in the exciting career of sales.

SOME BASIC PSYCHOLOGICAL PRINCIPLES ABOUT SALES

There are many psychological reasons why people decide to buy or not to buy. If you gain a better understanding of these psychological principles, then your performance will improve. You need to develop a deeper knowledge of yourself and the various types of buyers that you might confront. The difficult part is that buyers are not always aware of their own motives, or are unwilling to share them with us.

Because there are many different types of buyers, you need to vary your approach in different situations. Some buyers are very wishy-washy and are actually looking for a forceful, assertive salesperson. Others are quite resistant to any aggressiveness or coercion. Here is a list of some basic principles of psychology regarding sales:

❖ People tend to buy from people they like rather than those they dislike.

❖ Most people do not feel comfortable in high-pressure sales situations.

❖ Buying decisions are more often emotional than logical.

❖ People are not always what they appear to be or claim to be.

* Sometimes the ones who claim to be very logical are the most irrational.

* It is the overall package presented to the buyer rather than one single component that usually determines the final decision. Some factors weigh more heavily than others, but everything matters.

* Customers are usually appreciative about the common courtesies of life, such as gratitude, respect, and cheerfulness.

* Good listening and communication skills are vital elements to establishing the relationship necessary for making a sale. In fact, they are among the most important aspects of the sales process.

* Some people require time and an absence of pressure to make their decisions. Others really want to be convinced and sold.

* Some buying decisions are made totally on the basis of the lowest price, regardless of quality of product/service and sales techniques.

* People tend to respond more favorably to salespeople when they are in a comfortable state.

* It generally works against you to say negative things about your competitors. Focus on your strengths, not your competitors' weaknesses.

* Your ability to sell is directly related to your belief in the quality of the product/service. Obviously, you should be able to sell something that is your own creation better than someone else's. By the same token, you should do better at selling a service that you personally perform.

❖ Sometimes a customer will give an order to a tactfully persistent salesperson primarily to "get them out of their hair." So, consistent calling on a regular basis often yields business.

❖ When dealing with a sophisticated buyer who is aware of the common problems with your business, it is vital not to hide or deny problems. In fact, if you do so, you could conceivably lose business by your deception. Again, honesty is the only policy.

❖ It is important to be professional at all times, even when you lose an order. You never know when your competitor will make some mistakes and you will get a chance at securing some business. Be a good sport, and you'll eventually be a winner.

Keep these ideas in mind and refer to them often. Once they become internalized, you will possess a tremendous advantage over your competitors. Ponder these ideas, and consider the various ways they apply to you.

Index